CRY FREEDOM

Cry Freedom

*The story of Lida Vashchenko and her
remarkable escape from Soviet Russia*

Lida Vashchenko
with
Cecil Murphy

ViB

VINE
BOOKS

Servant Publications
Ann Arbor, Michigan

Vine Books is an imprint of Servant Publications especially
designed to serve Evangelical Christians.

Cover illustration by Jim Lamb © 1987
Cover design by Michael Andaloro

Published by Servant Books
P.O. Box 8617
Ann Arbor, Michigan 48107

Printed in the United States of America
ISBN 0-89283-355-6
87 88 89 90 91 10 9 8 7 6 5 4 3 2 1

Contents

Prologue: The Great Risk

WE APPROACHED THE NINE-storied American Embassy in Moscow at the intersection of Chaykovskogo Street and Tchaikovsky with the Embassy's red, white, and blue flag rippling in the light summer breeze. Four KGB men, two of them in uniform, stood near the front entrance. That didn't surprise us. In our previous visits, there had always been members of the KGB outside.

I walked casually toward the ochre-colored building, the way we had agreed. I tried to ignore the gnawing anxiety now coupled with a growing sense of energy. Eight of us, clustered in three different groups, crossed the street and approached the front of the building. The KGB men silently scrutinized each person but they did not move.

My two sisters, Lila and Luba, stepped up to one policeman and began to explain their purpose in coming. In an attempt to distract his attention while the rest of us came closer, they took out papers to show him. The man shook his head. "Nyet! Nyet!" He gruffly pushed them aside as I came closer in the second group. Not realizing that we were together, he turned toward us, giving us a look that said, "What do you want?"

My sisters moved back a few steps as if to comply. They glanced at us, giving the barest signal. I said nothing to the man, not even looking directly at him, and continued to walk toward the arches of the American Embassy. Someone started to run, and the air filled with shouts. Each of us raced wildly forward, determined to get through the gate and on to American territory.

The second uniformed KGB man grabbed for me, I ducked and darted past him. My breath was coming in quick gasps, and even though I heard screaming, I did not pause for the slightest backward glance. I kept running until I reached the Embassy doors. I heard yelling and painful screams but I did not pause to look back. Once there, I turned and saw that two men, one in uniform, had grabbed my brother John.

John struggled to get away but he must have known it was useless. Even though he was the tallest of us all and probably the strongest, he was no match for them. Their fists struck at him again and again, all over his body. "Let him alone!" I yelled uselessly at them. Mama, now huddled next to me, suddenly aware of what they were doing to John, started to scream. My brother's anguished cries rang in my ears and it was days before I could erase that scene from my thoughts.

"Stop!" I yelled. I stepped forward, not sure what I ought to do and not thinking clearly. "Let him go!"

John slumped forward, no longer resisting their blows. Father grabbed me to prevent my running back. His restraining hand reminded me that my gesture would have been useless anyway. The KGB would only have taken us both.

We had to watch helplessly while the other two men joined them and all four men struck blow after blow. They suddenly stopped and stared at him. We were too far away to hear them talk to each other, but one of them motioned to the others to help him as he dragged John's bleeding body away. I could tell he was alive but I wondered for how long. Tears streamed down my face. At that instant, I faced the reality that I might never see my brother alive again.

Sadly we opened the door and went inside. Personnel from the Embassy came rushing toward us. "What's going on?" they asked.

"They're beating our son!" Father yelled in Russian. "Stop them!"

For several seconds, everything was in confusion. None of them seemed to know what to do. The air filled with our frenzied cries in Russian, with responses in both English and Russian. Within minutes, the Embassy employees left so that only the marine guard stood before us.

Father walked over to one of the marines and asked to see the ambassador immediately.

"He is busy."

"His assistant, then. Someone of importance."

"He is not available either."

"We wait." Father led the way and the seven of us sat down on a long, comfortable vinyl sofa in a corner of the reception area of the consul section. I stared first at Father and then Mama. Their faces, drained of color, showed no emotion, only determination. I knew they, too, could not erase from their minds the picture of John being beaten.

One well-intentioned marine approached us. "Why don't you come back tomorrow?"

"If we leave, we can never come back." My father spoke with a surprisingly calm voice. "They will never let us get this close again."

The marine did not suggest again that we leave. He understood our danger. Throughout the rest of the day, various members of the Embassy staff also suggested we leave. Our answer was always the same.

That morning of June 27, 1978, marked the beginning of a long wait. We virtually lived on that sofa for a period of two months. We slept on it or lay on the lobby floor, but we refused to leave. We used their restrooms and tried to wash up as much as possible. Having only a small amount of food with us did not worry us because something more important concerned us.

That day, June 27, 1978, began a new phase in the struggle that my father had begun in 1963 when he naively decided to ask for permission to emigrate from the Soviet Union. He had been ridiculed, persecuted, fined, and imprisoned. This was our last attempt. No matter what happened in the American Embassy, we knew we could never go back to our home in Siberia or to any place in the Soviet Union. The government would make certain that we did not get another chance to defy them.

And so began our five-year live-in at the American Embassy in Moscow. Before long the world news media picked up our story and branded us "The Siberian Seven."

We told our story countless times. "We only want to emigrate so that we can worship God freely and without restraint." We had been saying that for as long as I could remember. Until then, no one had done anything to help us. Perhaps no one could. Now, as we waited, we believed that as difficult as our presence became for the Americans they would not forcefully eject us from the Embassy. In that fact lay our hope.

"If we stay long enough—" Father said several times to encourage us. He did not have to finish his statement. We pinned our hopes on seven Russian citizens' daily presence to force the Western powers into action. If we could not spur them to action with our pleas for help, we determined to force them to get rid of us.

One American dignitary pleaded with us to go back to Siberia. We told him, "We cannot just go back. They would never let us live in peace now."

"We will do everything we can to help you," he assured us.

We had heard those promises before.

On July 6, 1978, one week after we stormed into the Embassy, someone sent a telegram to the children at home but they did not receive it. Vera went to the post office to get the telegram but the official there chased her away.

Four days later, an official put through a telephone call. That brought results. He spoke with Vera and told her we were well and had refused to leave.

My parents got to speak to Vera. She told him that John had been returned home. He had been badly beaten and was in deep pain. The worst was a kidney injury.

She pleaded, "Don't leave the American Embassy! If you leave, they will do worse to you than they did to John!"

The Americans contacted the Soviet officials. The Soviets said that as long as we remained inside the Embassy, they would not discuss the matter. We knew that if we went out, they would take us into custody. Long prison terms and probably death would result.

We refused to budge. For sixty-four days we remained in that waiting room. We used their toilets, but nothing else. Eventually they allowed us to take weekly showers.

Americans in the Embassy, as well as visiting Americans, kept urging us to leave. We realized now that only by remaining inside would we have any chance at all.

To one persistent man I said, "We have already gone through so much; it does not matter that you do not like us or want to help. We are staying here."

"But—but you can't just stay here forever."

"We will not walk out on our legs. If you refuse to let us stay, fine. You must drag us outside and personally turn us over to the Soviet authorities for extermination."

He stared at me a minute, shook his head, and walked away. After that, no one urged us to leave again.

Father persisted that we had an invitation from Cecil Williamson and we would remain until it was honored. Maria Chmykhalov had no invitation and that concerned her, but she refused to leave.

On the evening of August 28, an American official came up to us. "Collect all your belongings and come with me," he said. They had decided to give us a more permanent place to stay in the Embassy.

He took us to the north side of the building and down to the basement. "In there," he said.

We saw the room, formerly used by messengers who stayed overnight at the Embassy. It was in the western corner of the Embassy. Through a heavily barred gate, we could look outside and see the street in front of us.

They brought in a refrigerator, stove, and what we needed for cooking. The room had held only two beds, but they brought in blankets so that all of us could sleep there. There was also a bathroom with a shower.

Reporters from everywhere came to visit us. Every time we had outsiders, it encouraged us. At least the Western world was hearing about us. We had no idea how extensively. We did not know how many people in England and America actively worked to get us out.

The days passed slowly. On occasion, the Embassy staff allowed us to place phone calls to Chernogorsk and we spoke with the children. It made us even sadder that we were apart.

The children were growing up without either parent. I know this troubled Father and Mama greatly. We did not know what else to do.

We had now come to the final impasse. We comforted ourselves with the thought that by the time all of this ended, we would be granted the right to emigrate. Or else—

We did not like to think of the alternative. At best, it meant a long prison term. More likely, however, they would kill us. We had no illusions about our choices.

ONE

The Christmas Decision

I SAT AT THE PIANO PLAYING for my two younger sisters the simple music the diplomat's daughter had taught me during the previous three months. It was December 24, 1981, the day before Westerners celebrated Christmas. We had already been living in the American Embassy for more than three years.

The Americans who lived at the Embassy had already given us lovely Christmas gifts and plenty of food. It had been a happy day—one of the best I had known since our arrival.

When I stopped playing, I looked up and saw that Mama had come into the room. Because of the Christmas mood that filled the halls of the American Embassy, I had temporarily forgotten the pain of persecution, the hardship of just trying to survive in Russia, and especially I had blotted out the loneliness. I had entered into the excitement of the biggest celebration of the year and had gone around all day humming Christmas carols. Looking back, I should have noticed that since early morning Mama had been unusually quiet. That was not like her.

Mama, who could be so jolly, looked both sad and peaceful at the same time. I stared at her, waiting for her words and sensed I would not like what I heard.

"I have decided what I must do," she said.

A strange sensation went through me. For weeks, each of us knew we had to do something to change the situation, but no one knew what.

Our basement room, located behind the barber shop, measured twelve by twenty feet. Its single window, at ground level, faced busy

1

Chaykovskogo Street. From this spot, we had our only view of the outside world. We had only to stand close to the window and beyond the heavy bars we could see the Soviet guards patrolling outside. Originally, there had been no glass, and when we opened the window for air, dust and dirt blew in.

At night Soviet guards tormented us. They banged on the iron grille to keep us awake. They shouted obscenities. They threatened, "We are waiting until you come out. It will not be so pleasant then. We will fix you so that you will never give us trouble again."

The Americans finally understood, as we had known all along, that our lives were worth nothing outside that building. As soon as our feet left American soil, the KGB would capture us. They were out there, all the time, waiting. If they captured us—I never liked to think about that—this time we had no doubts that they would kill us.

Father had been arrested many times before, fined often, imprisoned once, and had endured severe torture in a psychiatric hospital. They had warned him that the next time he spent more than three hours in the American Embassy, the Soviet Union would consider him a traitor.

Mama had served time in a labor camp. One of my brothers, Sasha, had been imprisoned for refusing to serve in the military. The state had abducted my two sisters and me from our parents several times and put us into reeducation programs. The last time, they put our parents on trial, declared us wards of the state, and took us away from them for five years.

When Father first started to protest, he had a single goal. He wanted to worship God freely and without harassment. After years of fighting for that right, and realizing he could never achieve it in the Soviet Union, his goal changed. He decided life would never get any better for us and our only hope of survival lay in emigrating to the West. By Christmas of 1981, Father had been trying to get permission for more than twenty years to leave the Soviet Union.

By remaining in the American Embassy we had received a lot of publicity from around the world. We believed that the wider the publicity, the greater the pressure on the Soviet government to allow us to leave.

Once everyone understood that we planned to stay, a constant flow of media people visited us. They wanted to know the facts. We told them everything.

A Dutch television team filmed a documentary about us. When shown in Western Europe, the label, "The Siberian Seven" became known everywhere. British author, John Pollock, taking up our cause, wrote a book by that name after we had been in the Embassy less than two years.

For a time our spirits buoyed. However, the Soviet government continued to show no interest in letting us leave. The Americans, as kind as they were, had no authority to take us out of the country. Even though the people at the Embassy treated us kindly, we sensed we were an embarrassment and they had grown tired of having seven people constantly around that they did not know what to do with.

The pressures were not just on the seven of us getting out of the Soviet Union. Of our family of thirteen children, ten of them were still home in Chernogorsk, Siberia, 3800 miles away. The youngest, Abraham, had been only four when we left. We had not seen any of them since. Naturally, my parents worried about them constantly. Because I was the oldest child and had cared for them during my parents' imprisonment, I often felt as if I were their parent, too. Dozens of times each day, my heart overflowed with loneliness and concern for them.

Fortunately, because the media people took an interest in the story of our refuge in the Embassy, authorities in our hometown did not harm the children as they might have done otherwise. If the government harmed them, the news would have leaked out and the entire world would have known. Yet that could change at any minute.

We did not want the world to forget us. If they lost interest, the Russian government could do almost anything to us. Remaining in the Embassy was our only hope, and as long as we stayed there, we were safe. But how long could this continue?

Although we were only seven people, that did not make it easy for us to live with each other day and night, month after month. We represented two families: five Vashchenkos and a fifty-year old mother, Maria Chmykhalov and her teen-aged son, Timothy. No such thing as privacy existed. We had differences. We had our share of arguments and quarrels. We lost our temper with each other, stored up resentments, had moments of jealousy; and, always underneath, we worried about our future and about the family members still at home.

We also prayed and sang together. We read the Bible. I was fortunate to receive piano lessons from a diplomat's thirteen-year-old daughter, Angelica, whom we called Angela. We began to pick up the English language. In appreciation, we did odd jobs such as sewing, mending, and babysitting. I assisted in the Embassy hospital. The work gave us something to do and helped the time to pass. We wanted the Americans to know that we did not only want to receive. By helping in small ways, we wanted to show our gratitude and to repay their kindness.

Now, as I looked up from my piano playing, waiting for Mama to speak, I suddenly remembered an experience of two months earlier. I had been praying, as usual, for God to help us. On that occasion, I felt a great heaviness in my heart. I began to cry and could not stop for a long time. Without hearing any voice or having an ecstatic experience, I had the sudden knowledge that a severe test was coming and that I would have to be strong. I didn't feel strong. Physically, I had been sick off and on since childhood. I prayed and I cried and prayed again. When I finally became calm, I knew that when the time came, God would give me strength.

"I have decided to fast," Mama said. "I will not eat again until something changes—until the problem is solved." She spoke the words simply, as if she had said casually, "I have decided to go for a walk." We had no doubt, however, of her seriousness.

I can't remember who spoke first or what we said. Her words shocked us. At the same time, we were growing desperate. Just that morning, we had been able to talk to the younger children by telephone. Alone and with no one to help them, they were losing confidence in our sit-in. Each day, the authorities harassed them, laughed at them, and made it impossible for any of them to work at a good job. Worst of all, they were on their own without the parental guidance on which they had always depended. All of these things were now having an effect. They felt keenly disappointed because nothing had changed.

"I have prayed about this for several days. To fast is what God wants me to do."

Mama used the word "fast" when talking to us. As Christians we understood her meaning. Later, when she talked to others, she called it a hunger strike. We knew about fasting because it is part of the teaching of our faith. Many times in the past when our family had reached the place of desperation, my parents and even some of us children had taken no food for several days. We grew up in a family where we prayed and read the Bible every day. Our parents had taught us from infancy that God loved us and would answer our prayers.

"Are you sure you ought to do this?" one of us asked. "Not eating—"

"I have no doubt this is what I must do. I prayed for a long time about what to do next. God has given me an answer." She still spoke softly but her words left no doubt of her intention.

I don't remember if we tried to talk her out of the fast. I do remember she said, "I think I will not live very long. I love my children and I would do anything for you. This is my last weapon. I do it gladly for you."

We kept talking about it and then she asked, "Will any of you join me?"

Luba, the only one of us who spoke English well, said, "I don't think I should. As you get weaker, you will need someone who can interpret for you."

"Yes, that is so." Mama nodded her head in agreement.

"I don't think it will do any good," Lila admitted. "We have been here a long time, and what does the world care if two women go without food?" She was so young and could not understand what Mama intended to do. Finally, she asked, "Mama, how will this end? What will happen if your fasting does no good?"

"We might die," Mama said.

That answer seemed so strange to Lila. "I don't understand all of this," she said. Mama understood that, too. She repeated that she would fast even if no one joined her. "It will be easier if there is another person. We could encourage each other."

I wondered if I should join her. I felt sorry for Mama having to do this all alone. I also knew she did not make this decision lightly and had been convinced that God wanted her to fast. As much as any of the others, I wanted the government to do something. "I need to think about it," I said.

Even though it sounds selfish, if I joined it, it meant I would no longer be able to take piano lessons. I would become too weak. I had never had such an opportunity in my life, and I loved sitting at the keyboard and learning to play. Yet in my heart, I knew I had to put first things first. I wanted to be willing to do that.

After a few more minutes, I admitted something else. "Mama, I know this means I am selfish, but tomorrow is Christmas. Our Embassy friends have given us so much wonderful food. Please understand that I will fast with you—after Christmas." Even when I said the words, I felt I was such a weak person, and yet I knew that I would not have the courage to go without food on Christmas Day.

She smiled and patted my shoulder. "Thank you."

We returned to our room in the basement. The Americans had previously used it as sleeping quarters for Embassy messengers. They added a stove and refrigerator for us, along with the things we needed for cooking. We five Vashchenkos along with Maria and Timothy Chmykhalov had been living, eating and sleeping in that room since August 26, 1978.

When we entered the room, Mama told Father she had talked with us and that she had made her decision.

A strange look came on Father's face. "No, Augustina, don't do this. It is not the way."

"I must. I know it is the right thing to do."

"This is crazy. You fast and nobody will care. So you die. Then what happens to you? To the children?"

"If I don't do this, Peter, the people of the West will lose interest in us. I must keep hope alive in us."

Father begged. He argued. Nothing changed Mama. Finally he grew angry. "I am your husband. As we have both read in our Bible, the husband is the head of his home. Is that not so?"

Mama nodded and Father started speaking again before she could interrupt. "As the head of this family, I tell you that you must not do this crazy thing."

"You are my husband. The Bible says you are the head of this home and I will not argue. But this time, I must obey God first."

"You cannot disobey me and obey God at the same time."

"I know what I must do," she said.

He reminded Mama that only a month before she had been seriously ill with colitis and high blood pressure. That had been a terrible ordeal for all of us. For days we wondered if she had cancer and the doctor had refused to tell us anything. Slowly she recovered. "What if you get sick again?" he asked.

"I will not get sick. I know it."

"But if you do?"

"Peter, then I get sick. But I will continue with the fast until—"

"Don't you know what the Americans will do? Before you die, they will hand you over to the KGB. You know the KGB will kill you." Several times he burst into tears as he used every argument he knew to stop her.

My fair-haired mother no longer tried to answer or to reason with him. Because she had prayed for guidance and believed that this was the answer, Mama would say nothing more. Father continued to plead but she held her ground. For a long time the words went on, but I saw that he would not change her. Father could not believe she was doing the right thing, and Mama would not back down.

She began the fast the next day, December 25, 1981—Christmas Day in the West.

Even then Father did not give up. "The Americans have generously shared their Christmas with us. Do you wish to throw this good food into their faces?" When that didn't work, Father kept talking about the lovely turkey and cake, the candy, and even cranberries. In that single room where we did our cooking, Father not only talked about the food as it cooked, but kept bringing items over to Mama and saying, "Smell this. Isn't it good food? Don't you want just a little of it?"

Each time, she shook her head with greater determination to continue the fast. Father was not being cruel. He, who had been so strong and had been the first to take a brave stand, had become different. When he returned from the psychiatric hospital, he had lost that fearlessness and boldness that I had admired so much from childhood. Whatever they did to him there, finally broke his spirit. He never talked about his experiences, but from others we learned of the tortures, the drugs, and the treatment that often drove sane people crazy. Once he said to me, "I would prefer to die rather than to go back to that place again."

I look back now and I think it was the most discouraged I had ever seen him. That was not typical of Father. He had always been an inspiration to me. Many times when I wanted to give up, he would quote a verse from the Bible or sing one of our great hymns. One hymn in particular begins, "The greater the sorrow, the closer is God." Sometimes he would put his arm around my shoulder and say, "Lida, we must never give up."

Father had held up and suffered most of his adult life because of his faith. Especially for the past twenty years, he had been strong and a living example when others wanted to give up. "Peter Vashchenko has endured. I can, too," I heard people say.

Father grew stronger when the government atheists argued with him. He had taught me well by his life and by his simple understanding of the Bible. More than once he said, "Lida, you must never do anything that goes against your conscience and against God."

That was the kind of Father I knew and loved. Yet this time, he held back, obviously afraid, while Mama took the lead.

Mama started her fast on December 25, 1981. On December 26, I again told Mama that I could not let her fast alone. The agonizing time of prayer and weeping two months earlier had prepared me for this moment. I knew God would give me the strength to fast as long as I needed it. "Mama, I will join you starting tomorrow."

She smiled and patted my hand. I knew she wanted me to hug her and to kiss her the way the younger children did. But I do not respond that way easily. I feel deeply within my heart but I had learned through my years of suffering under the Soviet system not to express my emotions to others. Now when I wanted to show emotion, I could not. I think Mama understood.

Father did not like it when I joined Mama but he did not argue with me. When I began the fast, I realized that in less than three months—if I lived that long—I would be thirty-one years old. I was an adult and Father had long since stopped treating me as a child.

Yet he did not let up on Mama. At night, Father lay beside her and talked of food. And, of course, I could hear every word. He still tried every possible argument to talk Mama out of the fast.

"Peter," she would answer, "this is what I must do."

"But your health, Augustina—"

"God will take care of my health."

"And what do you think you are going to accomplish by all of this? If you die, who out there will care?"

"God will care."

Listening to his pleadings with Mama at night, I sometimes held my hands over my ears so that I could block out his voice. I had begun the hardest struggle of my life. I did not know if I could hold out very long.

Again and again I prayed, "Oh, God, I wish I had another place to sleep, so that I don't have to listen to this all the time." By being able to get out of that room, I knew I could continue my fast.

TWO

Twenty-Eight Days

WHEN THE AMERICANS at the Embassy learned what we were doing, they also tried to talk us out of it. Their concern encouraged me. Their words, the way they looked at me, the questions in their eyes, showed they did not know what to do. If we died in the Embassy, they feared the Soviets would use it as propaganda to tell the world how badly the Americans treated us.

"Don't you realize what you're doing?" one official at the Embassy asked.

"Of course, I know," I said. "I did not make this choice lightly."

"But you can—you might—." He couldn't say the word.

"Die? Yes, I might die. Of course, I don't want to die. I hope that something will happen to prevent that."

Those words may sound arrogant, but I did not mean them that way. Once I knew what I had to do, it was simply a matter of doing it. Mama and I both reminded ourselves that God had not failed us in the past. We believed God would not fail us now.

From the time that people started to come and ask questions and try to dissuade us, I knew that Mama had been right in deciding to fast. That assurance helped me to remain on the fast. I don't recall that I ever doubted the path both of us had committed ourselves to.

We had promised to fast without setting any number of days. Yet I thought about the days, especially in the beginning, wondering how long we would continue.

Father's taunting and arguing became increasingly difficult to bear, and I yearned for privacy. Unexpectedly, a wonderful thing happened that I believe was an answer to my prayer. An American woman who lived at the Embassy went back to the United States for two weeks. She asked if I would like to stay in her Embassy apartment and take care of her two cats during that time.

That brought a lot of joy to me because it meant I could be away from the smell of food. By then, I knew I would have overcome the temptation to give in. Living there would also mean I did not have to listen to Father pleading with Mama to stop the fast. During the two weeks, she continued to sleep with Father in the basement, but she spent much of her time upstairs with me.

Mama and I decided that we would take only plain tea and no food. It was not enough just to fast, but we had to get the word out to the West and to the Soviet government.

I have heard people say that the first two or three days without food are the hardest because you think about food all the time. After that, they say, the desire goes away. In my case, the desire for food never left. Not for a day. At most, I would not think of food for two or three hours.

When I became desperate, I pulled open my Bible and read passages to give me comfort. One day I read about the temptations of Jesus. He rebuked Satan who wanted him to turn the stones into food. He said, "A man does not live by bread alone, but by every word that proceeds from the mouth of God" (Mt 4:4). Reading those words took away my desire for food for a few hours. But it came back. It always came back.

The American doctor insisted that we come to his office every day so that he could check on our physical condition. Dr. Shadler weighed us, took our blood pressure and checked us over. At the start of the fast I weighed 105 pounds and I am an even five feet tall.

Mama, two inches taller, weighed forty pounds more. Obviously, if the fast lasted a long time, she could hold out longer. She lost ten pounds the first week, but we knew that the daily weight loss would slow down. It did.

Each day I started out by praying and then reading the Bible. I tried to do a little work, but after a few days I quit because I tired too easily. By the twelfth day, I had grown extremely weak and it took a lot of effort to do the simplest things. I felt cold all the time. I asked for hot tea. My fingers and toes seemed as if they were always frostbitten. The tea did seem to help.

The kind Dr. Shadler offered us vitamins. "You will not gain any weight from them," he assured us. "But they will help you keep your health."

"No," Mama said. "Plain tea only."

I could see the disappointment in his eyes, but he did not protest. He wanted to help us and more than once I saw tears in his concerned eyes.

We knew by the second week that the fast was having an effect because the word had reached the West. Telephone calls, letters, and cables started coming to the Embassy. On January 15, 1982, we received a telephone call from President Jimmy Carter a few days before he left the American presidency. He expressed concern for us and for our health. I can never forget that he also said, "I am praying for you and I believe God will help you."

Senator Carl Levin from Michigan rallied behind our cause. He and Senator David Boren, along with their wives, had visited us in the Embassy late one night in August, 1979. "I will do everything I can to help you and I will not forget you," he promised before he left. The following year he introduced Bill S. 2890 that would give us permanent residence in the Embassy. Later, Senator Levin and fifty other senators signed a letter of appeal to President Brezhnev in which they requested him to grant us exit visas.

Reporters flocked in every day. They asked each of us question after question. They took hundreds of pictures. The visitors filled every square foot of the room. Almost without exception, they asked, "Why are you doing this?" I do not know how everyone responded. The Soviet dissident Andrei Sakharov had only recently undergone a hunger strike. Some thought we were trying a political move after his example.

We were not fasting for the government's benefit as much as we were giving ourselves to God. The two greatest powers in the world were pushing against each other. They caught the seven of us in the middle and squeezed from both sides. As Christians we had learned to trust God with no limitation on what he could do. Through many years of struggle we had learned that, ultimately, we had only God to turn to.

The second question asked almost every day was, "When are you going to stop?"

"When our problem has been solved," Mama said.

One day Boris Perthatkin and another man visited us. They came on behalf of the Soviet government and urged us to leave the Embassy quietly. During the conversation we discovered that Boris Perthatkin was also a Christian who lived in the far eastern part of the Soviet Union.

"Why are you doing this?" I asked him. "You are a Christian and you know how it is in this country. Yet you come here to ask us to leave."

With the slightest smile on his face, he answered, "I have come here to do what the government has asked me to do." He leaned over and said softly. "Now that I have done my duty, I can say to you, don't give up. You are brave people and you bring hope to all of us."

Another encouraging incident involved Ambassador Watson who wanted to help us. He went to see the Soviet President on our behalf. He presented a plea on our behalf.

"This is very funny," the Russian president said. "You come here where we can talk important business and you bring up a matter of little importance."

"We do not think they are unimportant."

"But they are of no great value," he said. "If you will put those troublesome people out of your Embassy, we shall take care of them. Now, if you want to ask favors, why don't you ask for somebody important?"

Ambassador Watson smiled and nodded. "In that case, if the Vashchenkos and the Chmykhalovs are not important, this is a simple matter. We can solve it easily enough. Give them permission to leave your country and we'll take care of this insignificant matter."

"No!"

When the ambassador came to see us and to tell us what happened, it surprised me that such an important man treated us in such a friendly manner. Only a short time before that, a Russian sailor jumped on board an American vessel and the Soviets demanded the man's return. America reluctantly turned him over. However, the world press made such a great noise over the affair that later the Russians sent the sailor to the West.

Ambassador Watson reminded us of that event and said, "Perhaps it is a matter of making a great noise once again."

At the time I did not understand his words, only that he was trying to say something to us. He said those words to us when we had been in the Embassy about two years. I later realized that he could not tell us what to do. Yet he understood that only one thing would change the Soviet government's position: a lot of noise from the world press.

During the days of my hunger strike, I often remembered his words.

We also met people in those early days who would be a source of great influence in our lives. One such person was Professor Phil Kent from Oregon, a tall, thin man with reddish hair who spoke Russian, and showed a great interest in us by his continued actions before the American Senate. Although he pleaded with us to quit, he never gave up on us. He had confidence that we would eventually be able to leave the country.

Keston College in England had been building up files for years on religious dissidents (we did not know that at the time), and had ready information about us when we sought refuge in the Embassy. They tried to keep the Western world informed about us.

By the nineteenth day of the fast, I could hardly walk without assistance. I discovered that if I bathed, I felt better. My skin became dry and scaly. I was becoming dehydrated. I figured out that by bathing, sometimes twice a day, I absorbed some water through the skin.

Each day I continued to see the kind Dr. Shadler. Each day I saw growing concern on his face. By the twentieth day, my weight dropped to 86 pounds. He shook his head slowly, knowing it would do no good to try to persuade us to stop.

After three weeks, the vice-consul, Kurt Strubble, kept asking the one question that touched Mama and me the most. "Do you really think you will help the children at home this way?"

We learned that our best defense was no defense. We were not doing this to change people. We were doing this, much as the Jews of the Old Testament did in times of great need. We did not argue. But we did persist. To those who really wanted to know, we tried to explain our faith in God.

I felt sorry for the vice-consul because he was now in a difficult position. He begged us to stop and told us our hunger strike was embarrassing the American nation. We kept telling him that we had no desire to embarrass him or America.

Mr. Strubble informed us that the Soviets were using our hunger strike as anti-American propaganda. "What if you die?" he asked me. "Don't you care about that? You're still a young woman."

By then, I was so weak I could not speak more than five or six words at a time. Even that much made me so tired that I would lie for hours unable to move after I returned to the room. I stared at him and said, "If I die, God can still make me alive again."

Another time when he seemed to argue relentlessly, I said, "If we cannot be free, I do not wish to live anyway."

Dr. Shadler's concern deepened. At first it had been about my health. Now it concerned my life. I had just gone through my monthly period and that weakened me even more. He and the ambassador asked the Soviets to send us to an American military hospital in Germany.

They refused. "If you are so concerned for them, give them back to us."

On the twenty-fourth day the doctor warned me, "You will have to stop soon. You will reach the place where it is impossible to bring you back. Your health will be in such danger that you will starve to death no matter what we do."

I tried to smile but said nothing to him that day.

On the twenty-sixth day, I rallied and felt stronger than I had in many days. I had the energy to talk slowly and in short sentences. That day I asked, "Do you know the story of a man named Jonah in the Bible?"

He nodded.

"You know, they threw him overboard and a big fish swallowed him. Maybe it is time for you to throw us away." I said those words because by now I did not care. I knew that although my will was strong, my body could not hold out much longer. I would die soon.

He burst into tears. "I can't! I can't just throw you away!"

His tears made me ashamed that I had spoken so flippantly. Yet, I meant every word. In the story of Jonah, the fish swallowed him but the man did not die. Three days later, the fish vomited him out at the seashore and he walked across the land. I still did not know if I would live, but I knew I was willing to die for what I believed in.

At each visit during those last days, the kind doctor ended up with tears in his eyes. His compassion touched me. Yet Mama and I could not give up. We had vowed to God that we would continue until the answer came.

The vice-consul, whom I had not known well, started coming in every day. He was getting increased pressure both from America and the Soviets. He pleaded. When that did not change us, he grew angry. I was too weak to explain or argue.

Back in our room on my twenty-sixth night, I talked with Mama. "What should I do?"

"You must decide for yourself, Lida," she answered. "You can stop or you can take vitamins like the doctor suggested. Or you can continue. No one can give you advice because it is something you must decide for yourself."

I decided that I would continue my fast.

On Friday, the twenty-eighth day of my fast, my two sisters helped me walk up to see Dr. Shadler. The stairs were the hardest because it took so much energy just to lift a foot. I had to concentrate and think about each movement.

When he examined me, the doctor said, "Tomorrow I must tell the vice-consul that it's time to give you up. If I wait beyond that, I'm afraid you will die."

He cried as he spoke the words but he knew they had to be said to me. He did agree that Mama, being heavier to begin with and not having the added complication of a menstrual period, could hold out a little longer.

Unknown to me, sympathizers in England arranged for a doctor to fly to Moscow to examine me. He arrived a few hours before the Americans turned me over to the Soviets. Both the American and the British doctor examined me and certified that I had no bruises or broken bones when I left the Embassy. This was a safety precaution.

At noon, the Americans called the Soviets and asked them to come and get me. Always alert to propaganda value, they replied, "No. You must bring her to Botkin Hospital yourselves."

When it became obvious I would leave the Embassy, Mama acted in typical Russian style. She packed me a bag of food she had collected from kind Americans in the Embassy. We did not say much in those last minutes together. I was too weak and I think she was too emotionally torn apart. But, again, she patted my arm, smiled encouragingly and whispered, "Go with God."

Vice-consul Strubble and three men from the American Political Office put me in a car. I shivered badly and they carefully covered me with blankets to take me to Botkin Hospital.

As we drove slowly through the streets of Moscow, I was sure that I was going to die. As I thought of giving up my life, it no longer mattered. My mind turned to my brothers and sisters without parents 3800 miles away, knowing that I would never see them again in this life. I remembered the abuse and punishment the government had heaped upon me. Father and Mama had suffered even more, and for a longer time, just to be free to worship God.

I knew then I would likely die. If I died, my death could help my family to leave the country because the world would hear about it. If this is the way God wants it to be, I thought, then I shall die but God will not die. Because God cannot die, he will not let my family continue to suffer.

I felt at peace.

THREE

From Our Beginnings

F OR ANYONE TO UNDERSTAND my story, I must go back to the time of my grandfather and explain the events that led up to our coming to the American Embassy.

My grandfather, Paul (Pavel) Antonovich Vashchenko was born July 28, 1888, in a village called Vaski in the Ukraine, and served in the army in World War I. Taken prisoner by the Germans, he remained on a farm in Austria for seven years.

Being Russian, he automatically belonged to the Orthodox Church. Among the Austrians, however, Grandfather saw a personalized kind of religion, different from the type of Christianity he had known. He became a convert before his expatriation in 1921.

While Grandfather lived in Europe, Russia went through a revolution and still suffered from civil war. Life had been hard enough as a peasant farmer, but it became worse when famine swept the land. Yet he managed to provide for his family. Although dissenters from the Orthodox faith suffered deeply under the Tzarist regime, Lenin's Constitution of 1917 separated church and state and recognized the right of every citizen to have freedom of conscience and freedom of religion.

In the spring of 1927, when my father was six months old, the combination of famine, poor land management and religious restrictions made living in the Ukraine impossible. Grandfather and his family left for Siberia.

By cultivating the rich land and receiving good harvests, the family lived well at first. Although a sparsely populated area, there was a variety of people, including sixty Baptists. Grandfather, partly because he was literate, became their elder and preacher. Eventually, Grandfather's younger brother and his wife moved to Siberia and joined them.

Because of Grandfather's determination to remain faithful to his beliefs, the government persecuted him. Stalin's Constitution of 1929 removed religious rights, and people could no longer propagate their faith except to adults. He also instituted the need for passports to travel within the Soviet Union.

During the winter of 1931, stripped of everything except the clothes they wore, Grandfather took the whole family and moved deeper into Siberia. Unable to travel on the Trans-Siberian railway because they did not have papers or money, they went on foot. The journey lasted almost two years.

Since they had no internal passports, villagers often chased them away. At the other villages, they asked for work in return for their food. The women and girls spun flax, did weaving, and washed clothes. The men (and by now several teenaged sons) put on roofs, built fences, repaired barns, chopped firewood, or did any kind of hard labor offered them.

They never stayed too long at any place because eventually the local officials learned about them. "You must move on within twenty-four hours." Authorities made sure the nomadic group did.

More than once they pleaded with officials to allow them to stay until spring because of the harshness of Siberian winters when temperatures fall to -50 degrees centigrade. The officials always refused. Starting out again, the parents carried the smaller children, like my father, in straw-lined woven baskets, the kind normally used to haul manure. They covered them with rags but the winds ripped through them anyway. Many of the weak and young died during that two-year trek because of exposure to the severe weather.

After nearly two years, they finally settled on the banks of the Kazyr River and that remained their home for the next nineteen hard years. The famine that swept across the whole nation included them. At times they ate nothing but birch roots and mushrooms.

Stalin's policies repressed Christians and it became dangerous to meet for worship, even in remote Siberia. Many parents stopped teaching their children about God.

In 1944, the state drafted my father, Peter Vashchenko, for military service just before his eighteenth birthday. In 1948, he met

Augustina Vasilevna Konovalov and married her January 1, 1949. I was born March 6, 1951, the first of thirteen children. They named me Lidia after a woman in the New Testament, although the family has always called me simply Lida.

The following year my parents left the Far East and moved to northwest Siberia to the town of Chernogorsk, which means "Black Mountain," because it was the center of a coalfield. My father went to work in the mine. Other members of his family came to live in Chernogorsk also. Later he changed jobs and worked in the automobile factory.

Church life hardly existed in Chernogorsk because the state persecuted all religious people. Some of them received heavy fines. Others went to prison. My parents held meetings in homes and they talked to their friends and coworkers in the coalfields about their faith.

My uncle Grigory Vashchenko moved about 250 miles away to Anzhero-Sudzhensk. Despite the persecutions under Stalin, a Pentecostal church thrived and many people joined, including Uncle Grigory. My father's two sisters who had lived with us went to visit Uncle Grigory. When they returned, they, too had become Pentecostal.

During the summer of 1953, Uncle Grigory and his family returned to Chernogorsk and he got a job in the mines. Uncle Grigory often talked about his experience in the Pentecostal church. He and Father frequently argued about the differences between the Baptist teachings and that of the newer Pentecostal doctrines. Within a year after Uncle Grigory's return, Father became a Pentecostal.

It had been bad enough that my family was part of the Evangelical Christian Baptists (the name given to the various groups that joined together in 1944). By embracing the Pentecostal doctrines that stressed things such as speaking in tongues and miracles for today, they were even more different and dissension arose. For the sake of peace, they began to meet separately from other Baptists and they elected Uncle Grigory as their pastor. The membership grew until nearly two hundred met regularly in 1961.

In 1961, Khrushchev started new persecutions against Christians. Officials told us that our church must register with the state as the Baptists had done. By registering, they promised to provide us with a permanent place to worship. We also knew that once registered, they laid down strict demands.

To register, meant among other things:

—The state regulated who could preach, what he could preach, and for how long.
—The church had to report the names and addresses of all visitors.
—No children could join a church before the age of eighteen.
—Church leaders could not give any kind of religious education to children.

The leaders of our church refused to register. They realized that because of their refusal, they would have constant trouble with the authorities. They were not disappointed.

Although aware of the consequences, my father was a man who did not fear the state. "I must teach my children the way of God," he said. He never deviated from that stance.

FOUR

Our Private War

K HRUSHCHEV PLANNED that within ten years he would destroy all churches and we would have total socialism in Russia. He began by trying to destroy the unregistered churches.

When our leaders refused to register our church, persecution began immediately. I was old enough by then to have some understanding of what was going on. In the spring of 1961, the KGB (State Security Police) arrested my uncles Grigory and Andrei as well as the assistant pastor, Andrei Miller. Uncle Andrei received a five-year prison sentence and died in prison under mysterious circumstances three months before his release. They sentenced Andrei Miller to five years imprisonment. Uncle Grigory received the severe sentence of ten years. He served the first two in prison, three in labor camp, and five in exile on the Mongolian border.

Arresting the leaders did not stop the persecution because it did not stop us from meeting together for worship. The government tried everything to discourage us. Often they interrupted our worship service. They grabbed Bibles out of our hands and ripped them apart. At other times, they came inside and shouted, drowning out the voice of the preacher. They knocked over the furniture.

More than once, they forced us out of buildings. We did not fight with them, but we did not move willingly. They pulled our arms and legs and dragged us outside. Fining us was another regular method because they knew we had little money.

They determined to wipe us out. However, we believed that God strengthened our small congregation to withstand it all. As we lived from one month to the next, we grew stronger. Father would say,

"Unless they kill every one of us, they could not take away the church."

The people of Chernogorsk joined in harassing us. Thugs stood outside our meeting places and struck us with crosses stolen from cemeteries. One time they threw burning photographic film into the place where we worshiped. The room filled with an acrid smoke that made our eyes burn and choked our lungs. We shut the windows to prevent more of these smoke bombs from entering. When we did that, people on the street banged against the glass and made such terrible noises we could not hear the preaching inside.

At other times, when we arrived, the locals screamed insults. "Fools!" "Traitors!" They spit on us and threw stones at us. They did the same things when we left.

A few members became frightened and stopped attending. We did not turn against those who left. We understood and we prayed for their courage to come back. It became more difficult for people to acknowledge their faith.

Although life was never easy, I don't wish to give the impression that we kept fighting fearlessly. Many times we were afraid and often confused. Yet, no matter how severe the persecution, we found the courage not to give in.

Finally, the authorities tried a new method: they went after the children. *And I was one of the children.*

My parents were active in the life of our country, helping to build the communist state. They tried to abide by all the laws of the land and participated in patriotic parades and carried communist flags and banners.

As persecution intensified, Father and others began to ask officials, "How can we work for you if you're persecuting us because we are Christians?" They received no satisfactory answer other than an urging to leave their superstitious faith.

As church members' awareness increased, most of them refused to vote or to participate in any state-sponsored activities. This infuriated government officials and labeled us as traitors who cared nothing for their country.

When I entered school at age seven in 1958, my parents had no idea how education had changed since their childhood. During my first two years, they seldom asked questions. They believed I was learning the educational basics. It did not occur to them that the educational system was indoctrinating us with communist concepts even more than they taught us math or reading.

One day I came home from school, singing a song we had learned that day. It extolled the goodness of the communist party and the virtues of Vladimir Ilyich Lenin, the greatest hero of the Soviet Union.

Father said something about not liking the song, but I don't recall that he forbade me to sing it. Although my parents taught me about the Christian faith, they had not yet reached the place where they understood that Soviet communism rested on the foundation of atheism. However, as Father became more aware, he started taking a greater interest in my studies.

One day in particular, I remember he read a part of the Old Testament aloud to the whole family:

> Now this is the commandment, the statutes, and the ordinances which the Lord your God commanded me to teach you, that you may do them in the land to which you are going over, to possess it; that you may fear the Lord your God . . . all the days of your life; and that your days may be prolonged. . . . Hear, O Israel: The Lord our God is one Lord; and you shall love your God with all your heart . . . and these words which I command you this day shall be upon your heart; and you shall teach them diligently to your children. (Dt 6:1-7)

My father had no real theological education and as I look back, I can see that he read everything and believed it in a simple manner. If the Bible said the words, he did not try to figure out any hidden meanings or question whether it applied to our time. His attitude said, "If the Bible commands it, I obey it."

Because he took this straightforward view, as did all the believers we lived among, he saw his duties stated clearly. "We are responsible for Lida's schooling," he announced. He quoted Proverbs 22:6, "Train up a child in the way he should go and when he is old, he will not depart from it."

From then on, he began a ritual. "Now, Lida, tell me what you learned in school today," he asked.

When I told him the lessons about the communist party, he said,

"You can no longer sing those songs. They are wrong." The next day, the teacher pointed to me. "Lida Vashchenko, you are not singing!"

"No," I answered.

"You must sing with the rest of us."

"I can't. My father says I cannot sing about communism or Lenin."

"Not sing?" She stared at me. "You must have misunderstood what he told you."

"Father says that these songs are not true. We find our happiness in God, not from following Lenin and the communist party."

I cannot remember how she responded. I know I surprised her because no child had ever refused before. Other children who worshiped with us attended the same school. They and their parents decided that they would sing the songs and listen to the lessons and the parents would teach them the truth at home.

My father would have none of that. "That is living a lie. We must stand up now for what we believe in." Father was a firm man and saw everything as either right or wrong.

From that day when I refused to sing, my teachers knew that I came from a Christian home. From then on, it would be a continuing battle between school authorities and my parents. They insisted on my learning from the approved curriculum. They explained that they only wanted to teach me values and truth. Father said, "The truth, we teach her. You teach her to read and to write." I did exactly as he instructed me. At that age, and just beginning school, it never occurred to me to disobey my father.

Father wrote to the Ministry of Education in Moscow. He explained that he did not approve of the songs they wanted me to learn. He asked for permission for me not to learn them.

The Ministry of Education replied that the Soviet Union had one education program, carefully designed to meet the needs of all children. Therefore, it would not be possible to make an exception for anyone. However, if the teachers or the education system thought they had won, they did not know Father.

Many times in school my teachers told me that I should stay in a singing class where students learned patriotic songs. Since my parents told me I could not, I decided to leave the class whenever they held those lessons. School began at 8:00 and dismissed at 2:00.

Some days I left as early as 11:00. At first I tried to hide in the restrooms, but that was the first place they looked for me. Once, the other students found me and forced me back into the classroom. After a few weeks, I ran from the school to my home, about a mile and a half.

It became difficult for me during winter because if I took my coat with me when I left the classroom, the other students knew I was running away from school. All students learned it was their duty to report anyone who did not conform to the rules.

On those winter days, I had only my dress to cover me. Winters are extremely cold in Siberia, often 35 degrees (F) below zero. Many times people saw me racing through the streets. More than once I heard them comment, "How can that child stand to play outside without a coat?"

I had no way to tell them why I ran without my coat. I didn't see any other way to escape the lessons. When I reached home, my parents were glad that I had obeyed them but angry that I came home without my coat and afraid I would get sick. Many times, they went to school to plead with the teachers but the situation never changed. The principal and all teachers insisted that I participate in the total curriculum. My father insisted that I not learn things contrary to our family's beliefs. At times, I felt caught in the middle, having no one on my side.

The other children treated me badly, insulting me, sometimes beating me. The teachers knew it but did nothing to discourage their behavior. The teachers themselves laughed at me. During classroom periods, whenever teachers had the chance to speak against the belief in God, they looked in my direction and added an unkind comment such as, "A few people still live in superstition, such as our Lida Vashchenko."

The words cut me deeply but I refused to cry in their presence. I wanted to show them that I was not afraid of them—even though I was at times.

When we had regular lessons, I liked the class very much. Each day on the way to school I prayed, "Please, God, don't let the teacher laugh at me or the other children beat me today." Some days they did not—those were the best days.

As schoolchildren, we were expected to join the Young Pioneers (the Communist Youth Organization) and to wear with pride the red neckerchief. Father forbade me to join. At the same time, he demanded that I study hard and bring home good grades.

In Russia, when children disobey a teacher, no matter how hard they study or how well they learn, their grades suffer. So there I was with my parents standing firm at home. At school, the teachers demanded just as firmly that I conform to the expected behavior.

Consequently, I brought home bad grades. More than once Father spanked me for my poor grades. I tried to explain to him that I was learning even though my grades did not show it. I don't think he understood—at least not for a long time—the impossibility of my situation.

Even though I did not know words like "depression," that explains how I felt much of the time. When people don't get help for their depression, they get worse. I became despondent when I finally understood that nothing would change. After awhile, I no longer cared if I lived or died.

"What do I have to live for?" I asked myself one day.

That day when I ran away from the school, I decided it was not worth being beaten by other children and punished by the teacher. I wished I could do like some of the other Christian children who played it smart. In school they did exactly what the teachers told them. They wore the red neckerchieves and hid them before they got home. They deceived both parents and teachers, but they escaped beatings at school and spankings at home.

On that particular day, I had lost my will to live. Instead of going home I walked to the train tracks and, looking around to make certain that no one saw me, I lay down with my head on the track, waiting for a train to come and to take away my life.

"What are you doing down there?" A woman's voice screamed at me.

I looked up. It was the track maintenance woman, making her rounds.

"I am waiting for the train to come and to run me over," I said simply. I didn't care who knew.

She rushed over and picked me up. That harsh voice softened and she said, "No, no, you do not wish to die."

My tears started to flow. I wanted to explain to her that I didn't want to live but I couldn't talk.

"Do not cry, little child. You feel so bad today but tomorrow you will feel better. Don't do this. You do not want your parents to be sad, do you?"

She led me away from the tracks. "Go home." She kissed me on the cheek. "If you come back and lie down on these tracks again," she said, her voice growing harsh, "I will beat you myself."

After that I was too afraid of her to go back.

Most of the year in Siberia is cold except for June through August. Because of the harsh weather and our inadequate clothing, I was sick much of the time. Finally, I became extremely sick and my parents took me to the hospital. All my joints began to hurt and the doctors told me that I had rheumatic fever. They kept me in the hospital two months.

When I returned from the hospital, my father did not know what to do. Finally, in April, 1962, he asked, "Would you like to stay at home and not go to school anymore?"

"Oh, yes, Father. I don't want to go back to that school ever again."

At that time he did not realize it but he began a war with the government. When Christian families saw that we persisted, some of them became bold and refused to allow their children to be indoctrinated in atheism. Most of them gave up after the authorities applied pressure. The authorities referred to us as the family of fanatics.

Although I loved to learn, I detested school. When I went they treated me badly. When I stopped attending, education officials started to come to our house. They put pressure on my parents. "Why do you not allow your children to go to school? Don't you care about their future? Are you so selfish you can think only of yourself?"

"She is not returning to classes," Father said.

"She has only two more months before school closes. Let her come back and finish out that much."

"No." He remained firm.

One time, the education officer asked me, "Lida Vashchenko, surely you wish to return to school?"

"I do not."

"But why?"

"The students and teachers are mean to me. Sometimes students beat me, but most of the time they try to stop me from running away from school. They knock me to the floor, then all of them sit on top of me and laugh at me. For them, that is fun because they laugh and push each other off and everybody wants to sit on me. It always hurts. Sometimes I cannot breathe."

"You must learn to get along with the others."

"How can that be?" I asked. "I am just one Christian child in school and that is why they torment me."

Once he got me started I told him specific things. They often played bad jokes on me. Once they put a dead rat in my pocket. Or they would hide other terrible things in my desk or inside my school bag.

The official left, aware that my parents firmly refused to send me back. Just as firmly, I refused to return. The official left in anger, threatening us and warning us that if we had any intelligence, I would return to classes immediately.

When the government found out that I would definitely not go to school they decided to take us away from our parents. In the local newspapers and on the radio we began to hear announcements that "some families foolishly cheat their children out of their right for education." They warned that any such parents would be taken to court and, if convicted, their children would be taken from them permanently. "Every child deserves an education," they said. Of course, this gave the impression that parents such as mine were backward and ignorant.

Father, anticipating that it would only be a matter of time until government officials came for me, made his move. He sent us (by now three of us had reached school age) where he had friends or relatives.

When the police came to the house, they did not find us. "They are not here," my father said truthfully.

"We shall search the house," they said. They searched thoroughly, but since we were not home, they could not find us.

"See, they are not here."

"Where have you hidden them?"

I think Father enjoyed saying to them, "You must ask me? Do you not know everything? You have all the power in our nation. You have telephones and cars. You will have to use those means to find them."

"But you can tell us—"

"I cannot do that," Father said.

This was more than a game with Father. He knew that such defiance could mean a long prison sentence for him. But Father believed he had done the right thing. When he believed that, he did not fear anyone's power. "God always has greater power," he would tell us.

"Stupid man! Don't you realize that we shall find out?"

I can only imagine the difficulty my parents faced. Mama reminded him, "Of course they will find out and they will make no exception for our family. Some day they may take them away from us."

Father did not want to think about that. He wanted us to be free at least until we were older and understood our faith better. He feared that if they took us at an early age, we would be too young to resist the pressure and would blindly follow their teaching.

At that time, Father refused to accept any further children's allowances. In the Soviet Union, families tend to be small. To encourage larger families, the state provides a stipend, beginning with the fifth child. Father correctly reasoned that if he accepted the money, it meant that we belonged to the state and they could decide on our education.

With Father's boldness as an example, a few other families withdrew their children. Maria Chmykhalov (who later became one of the Siberian Seven) had classes in her home, although we always studied with an awareness that we might have to stop at any minute and hide.

After months of hiding in various places, Father called us home. He dug a kind of basement in the house, and arranged it so that he could lift up the floorboards and we climbed down a ladder. When they shut the "door," they laid a lambskin on top of it and the police could never discover our secret place.

Although it was small and dark, we hid down there when education officials came to search for us. They came often. They knew all about our family. They knew where my father worked and the hours he would be away from home. Many times they waited until he was at work in the coal mine before they pulled up in front of our house. Sometimes they used as many as three police cars.

We played games like other children and tried to live a normal life.

Some days we outwardly forgot the threat of their arriving at any minute. But deep inside, we lived with the idea every minute of our lives.

We slept in our hideout and Father kept the door open. If the officials came at night—as they sometimes did—Father or Mama would close the door and cover it. Sometimes we slept through a search of the house above. At other times, their noise awakened us and we lay in the dark, filled with fear, certain they would find us.

One time, I lay in the dark and my heart beat rapidly. I could hear it and I thought the police must be able to hear it upstairs, too. The more I tried to stop my heart from pounding so loud, the worse it got. As a child, it was only the terror that made me certain they could hear the beating of my heart. It remains an experience I can never forget.

FIVE

Orphans with Living Parents

S INCE I'VE BEEN an adult I have often wondered how my parents endured all those difficult years. I don't recall ever hearing them talk of giving up. They disagreed—sometimes heatedly—on how to proceed, but neither Father nor Mama ever gave in or considered it as an option. We children learned by their example and gained strength from their lives as well as through their formal teachings.

I remember so many times when my parents faced the Soviets and showed great courage. I especially recall one Sunday when we met to worship in the home of other Christians. I was sitting in my father's lap when several police cars pulled up in front. Our leaders ignored the authorities and we continued with the meeting.

Police banged on the door and demanded in loud voices, "Open up!" They pushed the door open and walked inside. They hit people and called us terrible names. We still did not stop singing.

"You have an illegal assembly!" the leader yelled as he walked up and down the room. "We will force you to leave this house and stop this meeting!"

As they left the house, one of them threw tear gas down, although none of us saw him do it. Almost immediately babies started to cry and we realized what they had done. A few people left with their screaming children. The officials locked the door from outside. The man who had thrown down the tear gas banged on the door. "Don't lock me in here with these Baptists! Let me out!" They finally let him out.

Despite the tear gas, we refused to leave. They unlocked the door and came back inside, dragging us all out. They pulled some out by the feet, and grabbed others by the shoulders.

Once we were all outside and the officials left, we gathered at another home and continued our worship service.

Another time, on a hot summer day we had the windows open. When we sang, local residents heard us and gathered outside. The government officials did not like it. Non-uniformed police came and yelled, "Close these windows! No one wants to hear you Baptists singing and spreading your lies to the good people of this city!"

In the Soviet Union, there is no problem with people having loud music playing as long as it is not religious music. But when anyone tries to play religious music, officials stop them and fine them if they continue. Our leaders refused to stop the singing.

On a later occasion, officials came and demanded that we stop our worship service. We recognized the voice of the local mine rescue and fire brigade chief, a man named Sokolov. "You must disband immediately!" he screamed again.

We made no effort to comply and showed our defiance by singing a hymn. We could hear Sokolov order his men to strike the walls and doors as hard as they could. They caused a lot of noise inside. I suspect all of us were filled with fear, not knowing what would happen next. Of the seventy people in the room, not one of them moved.

Someone started a new hymn and we all joined in:

We are not given life for empty dreams . . .
So you and I must be ready
To serve Christ in sorrow and tears . . .

When we refused to stop, this infuriated Sokolov because no one resists police orders in the Soviet Union. For several minutes, we heard his shouts and the answering responses of the men with him. Suddenly it quieted down. We hoped that they gave up and went away. Sometimes—not often—it happened like that. They would harass us enough to disrupt our meetings and then leave.

At least ten minutes passed before we heard and felt the terrible crash against the wall. Sokolov had ordered the mine rescue truck to ram the house. Plaster fell from walls and the ceiling. Young children screamed. Framed Bible texts fell to the floor. The glass in the window shattered. I held tight to my father and peeked around. Several people looked as if they wanted to cry, but no one did. No one moved and this time no one said anything.

Nothing but silence followed for a few minutes, and again we hoped it was over. Then we heard the siren of a fire engine. It stopped in front of the building where we worshiped. Immediately, fire fighters trampled across the garden and raced to the broken window. They aimed their high-pressured hoses on us.

"Now!" The voice screamed.

Water sprayed everywhere. Suddenly everyone panicked and instinctively rushed to get out of the stream of water. Father, fearing I might drown, pushed me behind an overturned table. Powerful jets flooded the room and kept on until they had drained all the water from the fire engine. Yet not one Christian made any attempt to leave the house. Minutes later we heard the firetruck pulling away.

The people in our town turned openly against us. They either did not speak to us or else spoke roughly, often vulgarly. Former friends spit at us and called us "enemies of the state." We heard frequent threats against our lives.

"God is with us. Never forget that," Father said solemnly, day after day. He really believed those words.

At that age, I didn't question the existence of God. I was still a child. I tried to obey my parents. Only later would I begin to question Father's faith and the senselessness of all we went through.

During my childhood, while my parents fought the school authorities, Father also encountered trouble with other church members. Christians argued among themselves about what to do and how to respond to the increased pressures laid down by Nikita Khrushchev. Some reminded us that in the Bible (especially Romans 13) it says we must accept all governments as ordained by God. That meant we must even accept the persecution from the Kremlin as God's will.

Others wanted only peace. They said we should set a good example for everyone by obeying the laws and conforming to whatever the government demanded of us. Our faithfulness outweighed every other consideration.

Father said that while God does ordain governments, people bring in corruption. In Russia, we had reached the place where we had to decide whether to obey corrupt governments or to obey God. He pointed out that the Christians in the first century refused to submit to the tyranny of Roman law when it conflicted with what God demanded of them.

Almost alone, Father opposed those who spoke of compromise. Not one to speak in gentle words, he angered those who disagreed. They called him a fanatic and blind. My father answered, "God sends only good. Sometimes God allows evil to chastise us, to strengthen us, or even as a way to guide us from our evil ways back to the good. We must fight this evil from the godless Kremlin. And we fight to win. With God's help, we can!"

The local authorities must have enjoyed the division within our church. Because we always had spies among us, the police surely heard every word repeated. Yet, while we argued, the authorities exerted more pressure.

The members of the local church solved the immediate problem: they voted my father out of membership. He could continue to attend but he had to sit in the back. He kept coming.

Government officers spoke to our church leaders. "We want you to stop this Peter Vashchenko from causing problems and asking all the time for permission to emigrate."

"But," they tried to explain, "we can do nothing with him. He refuses to listen to us."

The officials did not believe the church leaders who were afraid that they might be imprisoned. Consequently, they came as a group to Father. "If you continue to cause these problems, we want you to know that we do not agree with you. Either you give up this fight or you must not worship with us anymore."

"I will not stop until our family has permission to leave the Soviet Union."

"Do you care nothing for us? You want us thrown into prison because you are crazy?"

When Father heard this, he said, "Then I will worship alone with my family if that is the case." He started worship services in our home. A few families, sympathizing with him, joined us.

I did not fully understand all of the events at the time, and yet I admired him because he never seemed to grow discouraged in his faith. Then one day the government decided to take the three eldest of us children away from our parents. Even then he never changed and he never stopped resisting.

I learned many things from his example.

"You have been in continuous violation of Soviet law which states that you cannot teach religion to anyone under the age of eighteen." Although I was only eleven, I cannot forget the judge's words to my parents that day in court.

That night I heard my father praying until late into the night. While I couldn't understand all the words, I knew he was crying. The next morning, I asked Mama, "Why was Father crying?"

Mama explained that Father was afraid of what would happen to us when they took us away from the family. My father was such a strong man and I had never known of his crying before. This made a great impression on me and I realized how deeply he loved us.

From that day onward, the state treated me as an orphan. They sent me to a home miles away from our town of Chernogorsk. They "sentenced" me to five years of education away from my family. That meant I could not be released before I turned sixteen. The judge explained that I would become a test case for reeducation. Since my parents had filled my head with many wrong thoughts, the state would have to work hard to retrain me and to make me into a useful Soviet citizen.

The next day, ten policemen and other officials came to escort me. I hid from them but they found me.

"Wait one minute!" Father said. "We pray first." Without giving them a chance to object, we all knelt down and prayed. John, then only a baby saw us kneeling and he put his bottle of milk on the floor and dropped down on his knees like the rest of us. In our custom, instead of saying "Amen," we bow and nod. John did that, also.

"See what they do to these poor children," one of the policemen said. "Even that little baby who knows nothing is already following the way of these Baptists!"

"We should take such people out and hang them," another said.

As they pulled me away, they kept telling me, "You see, your parents do not love you. If they loved you, they would not allow you to be treated like this."

Despite all the people around me, I felt as if I were totally alone in the world. At the same time I felt too tired to care about anything. I also realized for the first time that my parents could not protect me.

I hated Abakan Children's Detention Center where they took me. They had strict discipline. No one treated me with kindness or friendliness. Each day I thought of how I might escape to go back with my family again. Yet at eleven years of age, I had no idea where home was from the center.

During my second week at Abakan, Father showed up. I told him of the awful conditions. Authorities watched when our parents came. Knowing this, I determined not to cry or show how deeply I hurt inside and how much I missed them. My adult behavior surprised my father.

Because I was only a child, it did not occur to me to think of how much it hurt Father to see me like this. He held me and talked softly to me. He prayed for my safekeeping. Before he left, Father whispered that he would return in one week. "Watch for me. I will take you home."

The next seven days dragged by. Yet, knowing Father would come for me made it tolerable. Each chance I had, I went to the windows and looked out. I ached inside to see him again.

On the day he was to come it started to rain early that morning and continued all day. I saw him peddling a bicycle followed by a little boy on a second bicycle. They both wore loose-fitting, white rainslickers.

I went to a group of the orphans. "I have money. Let's go across the street and I'll buy sweets for all of you."

Excitedly, they followed me out of the Detention Center and across the street. We went to the store on the corner. As is usual in the Soviet Union, people formed a long line, waiting their turn to get into the store to buy things. I told the other children, "Wait your turn and when you get inside, choose what you want."

I waited until our turn came and as the children all hurried inside, I handed one child the money I had. I dashed around the corner where Father and the boy waited. Father pulled me onto the tandem of his bicycle and we were off.

The next twenty-five miles were mostly muddy lanes across the fields. Although a shorter route and one with no traffic, it was hard and tiring. We knew that as soon as the other children reported what happened, the police would start looking for us.

At one point, the river we had to cross had risen rapidly because of the rain. We had to leave the fields and travel along the main road until we crossed the bridge. We saw police up ahead. They stopped every car and truck and searched thoroughly.

Father, knowing they looked for a man and a young daughter, told me, "Slide up close to me, Lida." I got up under his floppy rain-slicker. He pulled my feet up underneath his seat and no part of me showed. The police waved us through the roadblock.

Father had planned what to do when we arrived at our home. If no nosy neighbors were around or if the police were not there, a friend was to stand in front of our house and light a cigarette when he saw the bicycles coming.

Father slowed down but kept me well covered. His friend struck a match and Father pulled right up to our house. I was home. Even before going inside, I felt at peace and was so happy. I was away from the horrible Abakan Detention Center.

However, Father had not told Mama of his plan. When we walked inside the house, soaking wet and exhausted, Mama understood immediately what he had done.

"You know the authorities will be back here to get Lida. This adventure will only add problems to the family. More searches, more overturned furniture and broken dishes. Maybe a heavy fine this time. Or they will find her and you'll never know where they put her."

In the Soviet Union, they sometimes take people and send them to places where no one ever hears from them again. Some areas are restricted and no one can enter the city without special documents. They have orphanages in such places and Mama feared they might take me to one of them.

Father had not thought of such possibilities. As a child, I could not think beyond the joy of being at home with my parents and with the other children. There were now eight children. I didn't think of the heavy load this placed on Mama. She was right and it was a foolish gesture on Father's part. But foolish or not, he did what he felt he had to do. Even though the government had told Father that he no longer had any parental rights because they had taken us from him, he refused to accept it. A stubborn man, this was his way to fight back.

Mama, being the more practical parent, knew exactly what would happen. The next day the police came and took me back.

One evening at the center, I was standing by the window. The last rays of the sun on the horizon blazed with a redness as far as I could see. Many times I had watched that sunset from our little house. A portable radio was playing and I heard a man's voice singing. At first I paid no attention because I was thinking of home. I wondered what the others would be doing right now. I wondered if they missed me as much as I missed them.

The song finally broke through my sorrowful mind. As I listened, I understood the sadness of the words and the melody.

Caravans of birds are flying home.
They are flying by me in the sky.
They are flying over me as if they wanted
    to take me
Homeward to my beloved native fields.

If only I could fly to the home where I lived
    and grew up.
If only I could rise into the heavens.
If only I could do that for which my heart
    longs,
I would part with my own soul.

You are my geese, my cranes.
Take home my song, my brothers.
If only you could understand
How difficult it is to be left away from
    the flock.

I understood that song. Even though I saw no birds, I could feel with the singer as he cried out in loneliness and sorrow. I felt as alone as the person who wrote the song.

"Why was I born to suffer?" I asked as my eyes filled with tears. "Why don't I just die instead of going on like this?" The pain inside hurt so much.

The words of the song kept coming back to me. I, too, wanted to fly home where I lived and grew up. As I continued to stare at the encroaching darkness, for the first time since being brought to that terrible place, I had a few moments of peace. To hear another voice sing the words that expressed the pain of my heart comforted me. God was near. Many times during the next twenty years I would face situations, some worse than this, and many questions would trouble me. Yet as soon as I asked why I had been born to suffer, I would also remember that beautiful melody and the words they expressed.

My next two sisters, Luba and Nadia, were also school age and the government tried to take them also. Father sent them away to stay in the homes of other believers and refused to tell authorities where they had gone. The KGB put Mama, Father, and my grandparents under surveillance. Within a month, my grandmother inadvertently led them to Luba and Nadia. A few days later, the education authorities also brought them to Abakan Detention Center.

Having two sisters with me made it a little more bearable. At least I was not alone. But I was not with the rest of the family, either. We comforted ourselves by remembering that Father promised he would come to visit us.

The authorities must have anticipated more escapes and decided to put an end to them. Without any warning, one August morning, they told us to gather our belongings. They put us in a police car and we started on the journey. Minutes after we left Abakan, we saw Father riding toward the center on his bicycle. We screamed his name. We banged on the windows. The policemen who sat with us, pushed us down on the floor and held us there. Father never saw us.

They took us to the train station and put us on a train. We ended up at the *internat* (boarding school) at Achinsk, 190 miles from home. Naturally, they did not notify our parents of our whereabouts.

The first floor of the *internat* contained classrooms, dining facilities, kitchen, and storage. Boys lived on the second floor and girls on the third. We lived among 300 children, one-third of whom were genuine orphans. Those with parents (except us) attended during the week and went home to their parents on weekends.

For six months, our parents had no idea of our whereabouts. They pestered local officials but no one gave them any information. They wrote to the Ministry of Education and received no response. Other Christians joined them in prayer, asking God to help them locate us. Although they tried everything they could think of to locate us, it was as if we had disappeared from the world.

Finally, Clava, a woman on the kitchen staff at Achinsk befriended us. She had no husband but many men friends. She drank a lot while she worked. The three of us were assigned to help her in the kitchen.

One day, I was peeling a large box of potatoes and started crying softly, not aware that she saw my tears.

"You don't want to work? Is that why you're crying?"

"No, not that," I said.

"Then why do you cry?"

"I miss my parents," I said. "I do not even know where I am or the name of this town and my parents do not know where I am."

My words shocked her. "You mean that your parents do not know you are here?"

I tried not to show my tears and held my head down. I could not speak but only shook my head. My tears flowed into the potato box. She came over and pulled me toward her and hugged me. "You poor child," she said. Then she became angry. "Such a thing should not be. Your parents need to know where you are."

"But even if I write to them," I said, "the government will stop my letters." Tears flowed heavily then and I couldn't say anything more.

"Somehow—somehow, we will find a way," she said softly and held me.

The next day Clava said, "I would like to help. But if I write to your parents and the government finds out—"

"Write to someone else in Chernogorsk, then," one of my sisters said, "then they can tell Papa and Mama."

"You can honestly say that you did not tell our parents if anyone ever questions you," I added.

"Even that is dangerous."

We pleaded with Clava. While she listened, she picked up a bottle of vodka and drank all of it. Drunk and with slurred speech she eyed me carefully. "Yes, I help." She took me with her to the post office to send a telegram to our parents. Clava was too drunk to write, so she dictated while I wrote the words down. I didn't understand what she tried to tell them.

The postmaster did not want to send the telegram. "This does not make sense. You don't know what you're saying."

"It is not for you to decide if it makes sense," Clava said. "It is for me to write and for you to send."

My parents received the telegram and even though they did not understand the message, they saw her name and the return address. They assumed that it had come about us. At least they knew where we were.

Immediately, Mama, carrying baby Jacob, and Grandmother Vashchenko came to see us. They did not have permission to travel that far but they came anyway. They contacted Clava.

Their presence frightened her. She knew she risked exposure if found out. "Go away. I don't know anything," she said.

"But you do," Mama insisted.

"I do not know what you are talking about."

Mama held out the telegram.

Finally Clava agreed to help us one more time. She left the kitchen and came out to the playground. Seeing me, she walked over and whispered, "Your Mama is waiting to see you in the field over there." She nodded.

We sneaked away from the others and had a wonderful reunion. After that, both Mama and Father visited. Once the authorities realized they knew where we were, they granted them permission to make the long journey.

Each time they came, they shared family news and listened while we told them about everything in our lives. Yet, no matter how many things we had to talk about, they never left without talking about God and how deeply he loved us. They prayed for each of us and reminded us that the whole family and the church members in Chernogorsk prayed for us every day.

Even though our parents had permission to visit us, their trips did not always work out so well. Sometimes after they had traveled their long journey and spent money for the train, the teachers refused to let them see us.

"They are busy with classes. They cannot be disturbed."

"We wait," Father told them.

"They will not have any time today or tomorrow or for many days to come."

Despite his stubborn nature, Father knew it would do no good to wait. He turned around and caught the next train home. Several times they went back without seeing us. Papa felt they did it this way on purpose to discourage his coming. Sometimes they got in, sometimes not. They had no way of knowing until they arrived.

One warm, cloudy day we were playing on the playground. I happened to peek through a hole in the fence and saw my parents standing on the outside. They waved at me and I knew they had been refused permission again.

That made me angry. I waved back and signaled for them to wait. I ran over to the principal who acted as the supervising teacher that day. "Please, may I visit my parents? They are standing outside the fence waiting for me," I pointed to the fence.

"No," she said and turned from me. She was an older woman, a chain smoker in her sixties, and she never smiled.

The other children liked for my parents to come because they brought me small candies or sunflower seeds that I would share. I called five playmates over and explained my plan. When I shouted, they would scream at the top of their lungs and each would run toward the fence, and like a starburst, spread out in different directions. When they reached the fence, they were to start climbing it as if they wanted to escape.

They did exactly as I told them. The poor woman, not very agile, looked in helpless confusion. She started toward one child and then toward another. She seemed unable to decide what to do.

Before she could collect her wits, I crept through a hole in the fence. I felt pleased at my plan and talked excitedly with my parents. By then, however, the teacher had figured it out or perhaps she saw what I had done. She climbed the fence herself and reached down to get hold of me. She created a humorous and awkward figure. She straddled the fence and then discovered she could not move. Her skirt caught and twisted in one of the slats and she could not pull it free. She screamed at my parents and at me, demanding to be helped and rebuking us at the same time. Between commands that I return to the playground and pleas for Father to untangle her skirt, it presented a ludicrous situation. Behind her, the children gathered around and laughed, which made her even more furious.

Father untangled her skirt. While she screamed at him, he bent down and kissed me on the cheek. "My visiting time was cut short today, Lida, but I was glad to see you if only for a few minutes."

I crawled back through the fence.

As part of my five-year reeducation program, I studied the socialist literature and listened to everything they told me. I listened and I repeated the answers they wanted. Feeling alone and away from my parents, I did not know what else to do. Inside my head I often questioned, *Is this wrong? Should I believe what they force me to read and to say?*

During the long years away from my family, I would forget much of what they had taught me. During my fifth year at Achinsk, questions would begin to trouble me. *What if they are telling me the truth? Is God real? Is God only a superstition, after all? Are my parents holding back the progress of socialism?*

In my confusion, I would question the existence of God, yet force myself not to decide just then. When I return home, I told myself, I would decide—once and for all.

Yes, the time for a decision would come, but first there would be five long years of emotional pressure and psychological manipulation. Would the years of remorseless and careful indoctrination "pay off" at that moment of decision?

SIX

The Question and the Choice

FROM THE VERY BEGINNING at Achinsk, the authorities targeted the three of us for special reeducation. They planned that through special psychological approaches over a period of time we would reject our religious upbringing and would become model socialist youths. They expected to satisfactorily accomplish this in five years. Moscow carefully monitored reports our teachers sent in.

The teachers, specially trained for this kind of work, spent a lot of time with us personally. The assistant principal, Giorgi Rublof, was assigned to work with me. He befriended me and showed sympathy for my situation. He was about thirty years old, dark, balding, and very large. He patiently explained, day after day, the lessons he wanted me to know.

"You see, Lida Vashchenko, parents who have not received a good education themselves sometimes attempt to teach their own children. This is a serious mistake, but we know they do it out of ignorance. They do not know what to teach because they have not learned well themselves. So, they teach superstitious things that we all know are not true. Superstitious things, such as a belief in God."

"God is not a superstition," I persisted.

When I argued, he did not express anger as my previous teachers had done. He smiled. "I understand why you speak that way. You are repeating what your parents taught you. Isn't that so?"

"Yes, it is," I said, "but that doesn't mean it's wrong."

"Wrong? I don't want to use that word. Let's not say it that way. If your parents teach out of ignorance, they are teaching only the best they know. They teach what their parents taught them. Isn't that so?"

"They aren't ignorant."

"I didn't mean stupid when I used that word. I meant that your parents have not had the advantage of a good education such as what the state now offers you. Your parents taught you well and you learned fast. And you do learn fast, don't you?"

"I think so."

"Lida Vashchenko, you are a bright girl. I don't want to try to force you to believe something you don't want to accept—"

"You cannot force me anyway."

"I know that." He continued to smile brightly. No matter what I said, he would not argue with me. "I ask you to do only one thing. Will you listen to me with an open mind? Don't decide I am wrong until you have had a chance to think it through for yourself. I do not think that is unreasonable. Do you think that's a reasonable thing for me to ask? For you to consider everything with an open mind?"

"I suppose it is."

"I would like to tell you what I believe. And it is not something that I alone believe. Everyone in the entire Soviet Union believes these things."

"Not everyone."

"Quite right. Almost everyone, then. Now, since so many of us believe, any fair person would withhold judgment and arguments until she knows what we actually believe. Don't you agree?"

I nodded my head. His questions troubled me, but I did not know what else to say to him.

That was the first step. Each day he taught me a little more, constantly showering me with special attention, frequently complimenting me on insights and on correct answers. Soon he arranged for private showings of movies that depicted the glories of the Bolshevik revolution and the achievement of Soviet science. I saw films depicting how the oppressed nations around the world looked toward Russian leadership for their answer.

Giorgi Rublof told me several times that Moscow searched for bright, young people like me to help them to achieve their worldwide goals. They needed my help to wipe out poverty and injustice.

"Lida Vashchenko, it will not be long until all the nations of the entire world will model themselves after our advanced socialist form of government." I remember hearing him say that and his eyes blazed with excitement. "And, just think, you will be part of that. You will help change the world into a better place for all people to live in!"

Giorgi Rublof's words made sense, and I felt a spirit of national pride welling up within me. At age eleven, I could help the rest of the world and make it a better place to live in.

I agreed to join the young Pioneers and to wear the red kerchief. I read all the information he gave me, and the more I read, the more he handed me. I had promised to be open-minded and to learn the truth. When I showed any resistance, he quickly reminded me of my promise.

My actions pleased him. The weeks and months went by. I did well in the special-study program they set up for me. I did especially well in history and geography. I passed in my mathematics but hated algebra. However, I loved my teacher and I did try my best.

School life became so different from my days at home. I received no punishment for not always having the best grade. Rublof only encouraged me to keep on trying. He complimented me on what I did well.

"Ah, Lida Vashchenko," he said once, "I wish I had two hundred more students like you! What a wonderful profession this would be if everyone maintained an open mind the way you do."

I read. I studied. I obeyed the rules—most of the time anyway.

All the while I missed the morning and evening times in our living room with the family Bible. At home, Father read to us each day and then we all got down on our knees in a circle and prayed together. In a way, it was strange that I missed those times with the family. When I was younger, I used to get bored and think they would never end. Now I longed just to be with them again.

One sad incident raised questions in my mind about Giorgi Rublof and what I was learning. I had been there for at least a year when my grandmother, then eighty-five years old, came to visit.

The authorities did not like us to have visitors, especially from the family, because of their influence. They hoped that by isolating us from them, it would help us to forget about God.

Grandmother, under great hardship, made the trip. She came to the building where we lived and she walked inside. Looking around, she saw two children in the corridor and asked them to call us. One of them went immediately to the principal and the other came to tell me.

I rushed to the door but it was locked so I could not get to her. I rushed to the fourth floor window and could see Giorgi Rublof talking to my grandmother on the porch of the building.

Although it was an extremely cold day with several inches of fresh snow on the ground, the sun shone brightly. I pressed my face against the glass but I could not hear a thing. The assistant principal was shaking his fist at my grandmother. Her arms laden with heavy bags, she backed up. From where I stood, I saw that he pushed her and she moved back again. He continued to push and each time she backed up.

He kept pushing her and I could see the fear on her face. She did not know it when she reached the end of the porch but kept retreating, one step at a time. Suddenly, she fell backward, her arms clutching at the air while her bags smashed to the ground and scattered their contents.

I burst into tears and pounded on the glass. My grandmother lay on the ground with small packages strewn everywhere. The assistant principal stood immobile, still shaking his fist. Finally, he turned around and went back into the building.

Slowly, grandmother got up on her knees and reached for the things she had dropped. For several minutes that elderly woman crawled on the snow to retrieve her belongings. Even though people passed by, no one helped her. I could see her knees were skinned and knew she must be hurt.

"Grandmother! Grandmother!" I banged my fists against the glass. I wanted to break it and to let her know that I was inside and could see her.

Just then the door to the corridor opened and Giorgi Rublof walked toward me. "Lida Vashchenko! Come away from the window."

"But my grandmother—"

"Your grandmother knew she should not have come here."

"But she's hurt!" I started to cry and could not stop for a long time.

"Your grandmother will go home now. She will leave you alone."

I cried, not only because of the way Giorgi Rublof had hurt her but also because he had been saying that my family did not love me. Almost daily he had told me, "They do not care about you, Lida Vashchenko. That is why they have stayed away. They do not love you."

I couldn't stop thinking about her down there on her knees and that Giorgi Rublof had pushed her. She went through so much trouble to see us at her age. Just paying money for the train tickets was a hardship for Grandmother. She had made a great sacrifice to come to visit us. Now they could no longer make us believe that our family did not care.

Now I knew without doubt that they had lied to me about my family. What else had been false? I didn't consciously think it all through then, but one day I would remember what they had done to Grandmother. I would see it as one more act of cruelty and repression.

Some days we played across the street in an area lot that once had been a cemetery. It was tree-lined and nicely maintained, and the city officials decided to put swings up so that we could play. Because the lot had formerly been the burial place for the wealthy, sometimes people uncovered gold, money, or jewelry. When putting up the swings, the workers dug deep holes and discovered an icon. Apparently it had no value, so the workers tossed it aside. One day while we were playing, one of the boys found it and took it to a teacher. "Look! I found a god!"

The teacher laughed. "Take it to the Vashchenkos. They need it. Maybe they have forgotten how to pray."

The boy and his friends took the icon to my sister and taunted her. She started to cry. When I heard about it, I grew angry and went to see my sister's teacher.

"You told the children to show us the icon because we have forgotten how to pray? You don't need to worry about our praying. We have not forgotten. We will *never* forget. Only because you do not see it, you think we do not pray." Once started, my anger spilled out. "We do not need to pray with icons!"

The teacher, shocked into silence, stared as I turned and walked away. A student told the principal what the teacher had done, and the principal then called her into the office. Some of the children were later told that the teacher had been berated for reminding us about God. The teacher was punished. Commonly, the principal either recorded mistakes in the teachers' permanent records or fined them with a salary cut, or both.

That teacher never joked with us about God again.

The government believed that their reeducation program had worked. Despite a few incidents which I assumed they marked off as childish or as part of the adjustment program, I pleased them. By the fourth year, I had progressed at a remarkable pace. I studied hard, got good grades, and participated in all the events required of young communists.

Giorgi Rublof continued to spend a lot of time with me, asking questions such as, "What are you thinking?" Sometimes he tried to record the conversation.

"If you record, I stop talking," I said.

He always quit. He may have found a way to record our conversation without my knowing, but I never saw a tape recorder again.

He encouraged me to study hard and I tried. When he saw my work, he always told me, "That is very good." Sometimes I knew I had not done well, but he kept saying, "Lida, you are a good student. I am pleased with your progress and so is the party. You are a good student in every way. One day you will sit in the front seat in our country."

He and others kept talking about my being successful if I would do things as they instructed. And I obeyed. I wanted to know everything and nobody studied any harder.

Near the end of the fifth year, Giorgi Rublof and his superiors in Moscow celebrated my reeducation. My chain-smoking principal received a promotion to a larger school, additional pay benefits, and a hero's medal. Giorgi Rublof received a transfer and promotion as principal to a larger school.

As my reward, they gave me a four-week vacation on the Black Sea. They sent me with other youngsters recognized by the state for their academic achievements. I loved those four weeks of relaxation and freedom at the warm sea resort. I was in the company of the nation's elite young people, and I felt proud to be part of them.

At the same time, a crisis was beginning to brew inside me although I tried not to think about it. I had grown to like Giorgi

Rublof. He had been kind and had shown concern about me. I wanted to please him.

At the same time, what about God? I pondered. My parents had taught me from infancy that God created the universe and that he loves us. I had moments when I tried to resolve the issue, but mostly I pushed the thoughts away. I could decide that later.

At the school, they let me know that I had a great future in store for me. I could enter a university and continue with additional education. I had thought of becoming a doctor, and now I saw that it could be possible because I could choose any career I wanted to follow. Those were heady ideas for me to consider at age sixteen.

One day, near the end of the five years, I escaped from the school because I wanted to see how my parents were living. I saw how bad their circumstances were.

"Mama, I am going to study hard. I can help make things better for you. One day I am going to be a doctor," I said.

"You cannot become a doctor because you are not in the communist party," she answered. "And if you do not join the party, they will never trust you."

"Then I shall become a judge."

"I think that is a good idea," she said. "You will be a judge and the communist party will give you cases against Christians for you to decide. You will then condemn them only because they are Christians and nothing else."

Mama's words shamed me and I did not tell her that I had joined the Pioneers. However, I now faced a dilemma. If I came back to live with them and declared myself a Christian, I could not continue to study. I would lose everything.

My parents did not question me about my beliefs because they realized that I had changed during the past five years. I could see the sadness in their faces, but they did not argue with me.

What did I believe? My parents had great faith. I had no doubts about the reality of what they believed. Did they have a true basis for their faith? What if they were wrong and the teaching I had received the past five years was right? What if there was no God?

I asked them questions that first day of my illegal "visit" home. "Father, how do you know God exists? What makes the Bible different from other books?" "Mama, why is this faith in Jesus Christ so important to you?"

I kept asking and they gave me simple, direct answers. As they talked, I agreed that it made sense to believe that God created the world. But that wasn't enough. I didn't have any interest in a God out in space.

Both of them quoted verses from the Bible and explained passages in the Old and New Testaments. But more than their arguments for God, they reminded me of many times when we prayed and God answered. I remembered that during the days when the government harassed us and our lives were constantly threatened, they had never given up. "It is our faith that keeps us going," they had said.

That evening, I took my father's worn Bible and sat down to read for myself. I started to read the stories about Jesus. At that point, I didn't care about his death or that he was the Son of God. I wanted only to find out if he was truly a good man. Did he help people? Did he care about those in need? As I read, it surprised me to see that on almost every page, Jesus responded to people who wanted his help.

I imagined myself living back in the first century. If I had been on the dusty road to Jericho and had spoken with Jesus when he came by, would he have helped me, if I cried out like the others? He stopped and touched each one who needed him and gave them what they asked for.

I thought of my parents and how they had prayed every day of my life. Not once had they ever shown any doubt about God.

I felt anger inside me. If this God is real, why does it happen that people are persecuted just because they are Christians? Then I realized that the government is the one that persecutes the people who are trying to do good. Then, I asked, if God does exist, why does he allow those good people to suffer such persecution? Yet if there is no God, why would those stubborn people follow him, even going to prison because of their faith?

The school authorities had kept telling me that Christians were bad people who worked against the government and against the great principles of communism. I did not know all the Christians but I knew my parents. They were good people. They did nothing wrong and only wanted to teach their children to do right.

My anger melted, but I felt more confused than ever. Who was right? Who was telling me the truth? I wanted to make the right decision, and yet everything seemed so dark and I didn't know what to do.

All my life my parents had taught me about God. But now I had to decide for myself. I could no longer believe in my parents' God. I had to believe for myself or turn away from religion forever.

As I continued to read, my eyes filled with tears. I knew the answer. Communism, even in its purest form, lacked the ability to motivate people to put the needs of others before their own. At the core, all of us have selfish motives and want to take care of ourselves first. I saw that only faith in God could take away our self-centeredness. That's what made Jesus Christ different. He did not give *to* others so that he would get *from* others. He gave because he wanted to help others in their suffering and because he loved people.

Even with five years of communist indoctrination pounding away at me, trying to turn me from the truth, I knew then that I could not turn from a God who loved me. I knew then, as never before, that I also loved God.

The next day I wrote a letter to the head of the Young Communist League in Moscow, identified myself, and told him that for the past five years I had been in a special study course at the orphanage. Part of the letter went something like this:

. . . I investigated the socialist system as my teacher asked me. He told me to compare it with my other beliefs. I agreed to do that.

I also told my instructor that I had no Bible to read and, therefore, I found it difficult to make a true comparison.

I have returned home and have followed through with my comparative studies. I have re-read special passages in our family Bible that explain what Christians believe.

To my total surprise, I have discovered that communism is lacking in many ways. I have completed my assignment and, therefore, I am returning my membership card and lapel pin. . . .

The education authorities and Giorgi Rublof who had spent five years reeducating me came to see me in my home in response to my letter. They begged me to reconsider. I did not yield, so they tried other tactics.

"Don't you realize this means you'll have no chance to continue your education? Your attitude will prevent your attending college. You'll spend your life in menial jobs."

"I must do what is right—"

"What you think is right at the moment. But if you think it through—"

"What I *know* is right," I interrupted.

They finally gave up. Giorgi lost his position and the generous pay raise he had received. Worse, the Ministry of Education demoted him to being a classroom teacher again and transferred him to a school in one of the lesser districts. We heard that he began to drink heavily and had many problems in his life.

After the failure to reeducate me, the teachers changed in their treatment of my sisters. I had been under the system much longer and they had not changed me. What chance did they have with the other two? Previously, they had not ridiculed their religion or treated them badly. Now they saw that the great educational dream had failed.

"If you don't like it here," a teacher said to them one day, "why don't you just go home? We don't need you here."

From that moment on, my sisters slowly began to realize that they could go home. They finally left.

I'm happy to add that all three of us girls came away from the orphanage stronger Christians than when we went in. Both of my sisters went through similar periods of crisis when they had to make the choice about what they actually believed.

Sadly, not all of the other Christian families whose children went through the same kind of program made the same choice.

SEVEN

Father's Decision

THE BATTLE NEVER STOPPED between the Soviet officials and my parents. At times the strife diminished only to erupt again with a new frenzy of problems.

Father insisted, "We want only to worship God in peace. What can be wrong with that? We are willing to be good citizens and to obey the laws, but we will not bow to anyone but the true God."

Another issue they argued back and forth about was education. Father said, "You communists teach your children what you believe. I also wish to teach mine what I believe. I want a religious school for my children."

"Do you wish to turn back to how it was in this country before 1917?" (Under the Tzar, Russia had parochial schools.)

"I want schooling for my children where the system does not undermine what we parents teach them."

"If you insist on a religious school, it is better if you emigrate."

"Yes, perhaps that is best," Father said.

Until that time, about 1960, Father had not thought of emigration. The government officials put the idea into his head when they argued with him about education. It was an idea that occupied his thoughts for a long time.

Finally, Father reached a decision. One day he said to Mama and the whole family, "We are going to emigrate from the Soviet Union."

That decision may sound like a simple and obvious conclusion, but it sounded unreasonable to many. At that time, my parents had the responsibility of seven children and my father's parents. We were poor people with no resources for money. With no political contacts and nowhere to go, it seemed insane. But that did not stop my strong-minded father. In his mind, it was settled. He did not know how or when it would happen, but he believed that one day we would leave our homeland to go to a place where we could worship in freedom.

Father went through the proper steps to obtain exit visas. For years, however, he could not even get the forms to fill out. Many times he petitioned the government. Mostly he received no response. A few times, government officials tried to reason with us or told him to stop troubling them.

"We must do something. Something drastic," Father said, "if we are ever to get permission to leave the Soviet Union."

I was seventeen then and out of the orphanage. Father's drastic step was to ask the Americans for help. He had tried that before and gotten no results. Yet he believed that if he could just find a way to talk to the American ambassador and explain our situation, he would help. Father decided to take me along, and after considering the situation, also my sisters Luba (age fifteen), Nadia (thirteen) and Vera (twelve).

As an example of his determination, Father had to sell our milk cow to get enough money for all of us to go by train to Moscow.

Upon arrival at Belorussia Railway Station on May 29, 1968, we went immediately to the American Embassy. Father and I had discussed the procedure at length. We knew that we could not merely walk up to the Embassy and go inside. The KGB agents stationed outside prevented people like us from getting in.

We would come close and then make a run for it. We told the children that when we reached the Embassy, they were to run to the front entrance and to try to get inside.

As soon as we approached, alert KGB agents grabbed Father and me and dragged us back. The children dodged their captors and raced inside.

Unfortunately, they did not speak any English. Luba knew one sentence in English: "We want to see the ambassador." The girls raced down the hall and Luba spoke her single sentence to anyone who would listen. Naturally, she did not understand their responses. Finally, two American women in an office called a Russian employee to speak to them. When the Russian discovered that the police detained us outside, he took the children into the hallway and forced them outside and turned them over to the police.

The police took us all to a nearby station. They presumed, without asking, that Father and I were husband and wife and that the children were ours. They questioned Father in a room down the hall. He did not have an internal passport to travel and had, therefore, broken another law as well. When questioned, he told his interrogators exactly why we had come to Moscow. They questioned me separately, but I refused to tell them anything.

The man who questioned me kept at it for over an hour. He grew angry when I refused to give him clear answers. In exasperation, he pulled out his pistol and pointed it at me. "Do you know what this is?"

"A gun."

"With this gun I could kill you. Do you know that?"

"Yes."

He stuck the gun in my ear. "If you do not answer my questions, I will kill you!"

"It's all right," I said. "Pull the trigger if you like. I have lived long enough."

My answer unnerved him. It is not usual in the Soviet Union for people to defy authority, especially when threatened. Without another word, he walked out of the room. That ended the interview.

They transferred all four of us girls to the Danilovsky Children's Center. We remained there until June 18, 1968. Quite late that evening they lied to us and told us we were returning home. Instead, the government flew us to Krasnoyarsk, the provincial capital. On the plane, we had several guards with us. The woman guard in charge tried to get us to talk to her, but that only made us more determined to remain silent.

At one point, because of air turbulence, the plane dropped sharply and scared most of us. I stared at the woman; she had turned pale and was twisting her hands anxiously. She turned to me, "Don't be afraid. We will be all right soon."

"I'm not afraid. I want this plane to crash and to end all of our suffering."

"Surely not!" she said without thinking. I saw the fear on her face and realized her fear of death.

I meant those words. I was so tired of fighting each day of my life and I didn't want any more of it. Dying seemed a peaceful solution. It gave me some peace to know that if the plane should crash, it would be all right because I was ready to die.

We had no further trouble and landed at Krasnoyarsk airport. Our guards took us to the Children's Holding Center. On the ride to the Holding Center, I asked about our parents.

One of the guards laughed. "You no longer have a family. Your father is in prison. Your mother is in prison and your aunt is in prison. The other children have been taken from the house and put into children's institutions."

I did not want to believe his words, and I had learned they would tell me what they wanted me to hear. I said nothing but I felt as if my heart had been cut out and thrown away.

When they gave us beds, I lay in silence but prayed for God's help. I did not know if I could go on living if my parents and all my brothers and sisters had been taken away.

Even though I had no desire to live, I survived and many days I wondered why.

After a few weeks they transferred us to Kansk, about one hundred thirty miles from Krasnoyarsk. It was as if I now relived much of my life over. Day followed day and I fit into the routine but always I determined to run away. I did not get my chance to leave until September 20. On that day I received permission to walk into the city. I had a little money and I used it for a train ticket home. I had been gone four months and was so happy to be home. But Mama, Father, and Aunt Natasha were no longer there.

As we later learned the story, the officials released Father on June 6, 1968, one week after the five of us had been arrested at the American Embassy. They sent him home with a warning never to go near the American Embassy again. If he did, they would treat him as a traitor and threatened, "We assure you that you will go to prison for a long, long time." Father knew it was no idle threat.

When Father returned home, he explained what happened. He, Mama, and my Aunt Natasha decided that they should all go back to Moscow and work to get us freed. Even though common sense warned him that appealing to the government for help would accomplish nothing, that did not stop him. Father's faith in God and his love for us gave him the boldness to risk imprisonment by going back. Again, he decided they should go directly to the American Embassy on our behalf. Hurriedly they made arrangements with other Christian families to take in the children who remained at home. Then they left once again for Moscow.

On the morning of June 18, 1968 (the same day we four girls were flown to Krasnoyarsk), the three of them approached the American Embassy. Father tried to explain why he had returned. The guard refused him entrance, but somehow Father managed to get past the guards, although they grabbed Mama and Aunt Natasha.

Once inside, Father talked to the American ambassador, Llewellyn Thompson. He tried to help Father by making telephone calls to find out where they had taken us. The authorities told him that we were being held at the Danilovsky Children's Center. The Americans drove Father to the center in a diplomatic car. However, when they arrived, the head of the center denied that we were there. Actually, we didn't leave for another ten hours after Father's visit.

Officials at the center said, "We do not kidnap little girls. Why should we keep them here? Don't you know where they are?"

"Of course we don't. You arrested them—"

"Respectable parents know the whereabouts of their family members. What kind of father are you?"

"Please," he pleaded, "I want my daughters back."

"Because you brought them to Moscow and they had no money and no food, we had to send them back to their home in Siberia. Because we care for our citizens, we sent them back at the expense of the state." The man finished by lecturing Father for being a poor parent and for abandoning his children.

Back at the Embassy, Father talked to the ambassador about emigrating from Russia to settle in the United States and asked for his help. He left with forms to fill out to immigrate to America.

As soon as Father left the Embassy and stepped off American soil, the KGB arrested him. They took him, Mama, and Aunt Natasha to the Eleventh Police Sector where they confiscated the papers he had received from Ambassador Thompson. Father remained separated from the two women.

The state tried my parents. They sentenced Father to two months in a psychiatric hospital, located at 15 Karshirsk Highway in Moscow, with the remaining sentence after his "treatment" to be served at a labor camp near Reshoty. I know few details of his time in the psychiatric hospital except that they labeled him as dangerous, forced him to take various kinds of medication every day, and gave him terrible treatment. I have always believed that they did something to him at the hospital that no threats or punishment had ever managed to do before. Whatever they did, it finally affected him. They never destroyed his faith; they did steal his courage.

Mama and Aunt Natasha both received three years in a labor camp.

Back at home, the burden of the family fell upon me. My sisters Luba, Nadia, and Vera were still at Kansk. My grandparents were at home with me, but they were both elderly and could not do much. I had to oversee the remaining children and get a job to bring in money for food and necessities.

Because of my refusal to remain in the Young Communist League, I could find jobs only at the lowest level. Finally, I did get a job in the coal mine. For eight hours each day I shoveled coal. I weighed 100 pounds and had never been physically strong. They used outdated and poorly taken-care-of equipment. The large bin into which I shoveled often broke down. I would have to stand and watch the lumps come thundering back down at me. I waited for them to repair the equipment and I started again.

It was hard work and it took so much out of me each time I lifted a load of coal, I thought each would be my last one. Yet I had to continue to work to support the rest of the family. I kept the job as long as I could.

I didn't know what to do. I came home exhausted and had to make decisions for the family. Being the oldest at seventeen, I know now that I made many wrong decisions and sometimes was too tired to oversee the house properly. I did the best I could.

It became apparent that I could not survive in the coal mine long. I was always cold, often wet. Many days I went to work sick; by the time I returned home, I could only clean the coal dust from my body and fall across my bed. I felt guilty for being weak. I lay in bed and cried in the darkness many nights because I was not doing an adequate job of taking care of the younger ones.

Even so, it soon became too much to bear. Many times I cried out,

"Oh, God, how long do we have to go on like this? Must it always be like this?"

Then I would think of Mama and Aunt Natasha in the labor camp and Father in the psychiatric hospital. They had no one. At least I had brothers, sisters, and grandparents with me.

EIGHT

The Visits

I WAS SEVENTEEN IN 1968 when Mama received the three-year sentence in a collective labor camp. My Aunt Natasha, quite ill with asthma, went to a labor camp for invalids. Her health continued to deteriorate. She was never well again and died during our first months in the American Embassy in Moscow.

In November, 1969, the state sent Mama to Mozhaisk, about six hundred miles from Chernogorsk and in a much colder area. The camp lay inside a massive barbed-wire fence. She lived in a barracks and worked in the sewing factory for long hours every day.

When I first returned to Chernogorsk, I had to go to the homes of various Christians where my parents had left the other children. I knew that at any time I could be arrested for having walked out of the *internat* at Kansk. But I knew I had not been properly sentenced and that, at seventeen, they had no right to keep me. Strangely enough, no one ever tried to take me back.

Members of the Chernogorsk education committee kept demanding that I voluntarily send the older children to an *internat* and the younger ones to a home. "If you don't care about yourself, at least let the little ones have their chance in life," they said.

My own bitter memories enabled me to say, "We can manage everything here."

"But if you turn the children over to us, they will have a chance to live a good life and become good citizens—"

"We will keep all of the children here and we will manage." I held Pavel, barely one year old, and defied the authorities. Although they kept asking for the children, they did nothing to take them by force.

If I had given them up, they would have used this as propaganda and said, "You see, she gave them up. She did not want them."

When we finally received a letter from Mama, it brought both joy to our hearts and tears to all our eyes. She missed us all and she had no one to visit her. She did not ask for anyone to come but told of her loneliness and how she constantly thought of each of us throughout each day.

I remembered my own days and nights of isolation from my sisters in the *internat* at Kansk. "It must be hard for Mama," I told the others when I finished reading her letter. I had to fight away the tears that wanted to flow.

Right then I made up my mind that I would make the long journey to visit her. Church friends again helped by welcoming the children into their homes.

Normally, I would not have had the money to make such a trip. I reapplied for the stipend for children. When the money came, I used most of it to take the train to Moshaisk.

I went alone, carrying a large suitcase filled with food because in prison they fed prisoners poorly. When I got on the train, the female conductor guided me to a *kupe* (a compartment for four people) to sit with two elderly women and a man. The man smiled at me but I ignored him. Every time I glanced his way, his eyes were on me and I felt uncomfortable.

Two hours later, the elderly women got off the train. The man left the *kupe* and I hoped he was getting off, too. He returned shortly, closed the compartment door and smiled as he said, "We won't be disturbed in here."

Coming from my sheltered background, I knew little about the ways of the world and it took several minutes before it occurred to me what he meant.

"I bribed the conductor," he said. "We can be alone for the rest of the trip."

I was too frightened and too confused to answer. I avoided his gaze. He came over and sat down beside me. I inched away from him.

"Shy, are you?"

I moved to the corner and felt fear crawling inside of me. "Please don't come closer," I said.

"I am too far away," he said and inched closer. He laid his hand on my shoulder and pulled me toward him. He was a large man and strong. I tried to push him away but that didn't discourage him. He leaned forward to kiss me.

I jerked my head away and struck him on the chest. "Leave me alone!"

"None of that!"

"Let me go!" I screamed. At the same time, I kicked, struck him in the chest and tried to push him away.

He seemed to enjoy my resistance. "You're a fighter, I think," he said as he pulled me close again but I still fought. He ripped the front of my dress and in the ensuing fight, I bit him on the mouth.

"Leave me alone! I won't give in!" I continued to kick and scream. I finally pushed him away.

He let me go, staring at me as if amazed that I would fight him. While he hesitated in confusion as to what he should do next, I rushed to the door and dashed out of the compartment. I raced down the passageway until I found the conductor.

After I told her my story, she said, "What do you expect? He is a man. You are a woman."

"I did not expect him to attack me."

"If I had a daughter your age on the train, I would be honored that he wanted her. Go back and enjoy it."

I could hardly believe her words. "I will not go back there!"

"Suit yourself," she said and moved on.

"But—but where can I go?"

"Why should that be my problem?" She went to the next car.

I walked down the corridor. The only other compartment I could find that did not already have four people was one occupied by three soldiers. I hesitated a long time and prayed silently for help before I opened the door.

"Please," I explained, "I need a place to stay and—and I'm very much afraid." I stood in the corridor and talked and they listened while I told them what happened.

"Don't worry," one of them said as he invited me inside. "We will be like your brothers and we promise to take care of you. No one will harm you."

Although it could have been a trick, I believed the soldier spoke sincerely; I came inside and felt as safe with them as if I shared the *kupe* with my own brothers.

A few minutes later, we heard noise in the hallway. One of them peeked out of the compartment and saw the man coming our way. He was knocking on every door, demanding that I come out.

"Quick," the soldier said. "Up here." He lifted me up to the top sleeper which had not been opened. Because I am small, he pushed me against the wall, stuck two pillows in front of me, and lay down.

"Where is she?" The man barged into the compartment. "The small-sized girl?"

"Do you see her here?" one of them asked.

He surveyed the room, swore under his breath, and said, "I heard she came into this *kupe*." He closed the door and moved on.

I thought about my purse and my belongings. All my money and my papers were in that compartment. The soldiers told me to sleep well and they would walk down there with me in the morning to retrieve my possessions. Again, I believed them, and I slept soundly.

The next morning, about an hour before we reached Mozhaisk, they accompanied me back to the compartment. One of them opened the door, walked inside, picked up my things, and said nothing to the man.

Just as we walked away, the conductor saw us. "Ah, this is quite a girl, this one from Siberia. She did not like the nice gentleman back there but instead wanted to sleep with three!" She walked on, laughing.

Naturally, it offended me. Before I could reply, one of the soldiers said, "She is a stupid cow, Lida. Why do you care about what she said? We know the truth."

"And so does God," I said, and thanked them.

When I arrived at Mozhaisk, someone showed me how to get to the women's labor camp. When I arrived, the woman officer did not want to let me come in because I had not written for permission to visit.

"I did not realize I needed a permit."

"You must have written permission for me to let you inside to see a prisoner."

"Please," I begged, "I promise not to violate the rule again. I have come so far and I am so tired. My mother has been here a long time and she has not had a single visitor."

She kept repeating the rules, but I had a feeling that she wanted to help me.

"Please, this one time only."

She stared at me as if trying to make up her mind. "Two hours," she finally said. "I will give you that much this time. But you must have the presence of an escort."

"That does not matter. I only want to see my mother."

She called a uniformed woman who escorted me down a long hallway and into one of several small rooms. She called it the common room. "Sit." She pointed to a chair behind a table and left. I waited a long time, perhaps a full hour, before they brought her.

Mama came into the room and stopped. She looked around and I'm not sure she recognized me at first, or perhaps she was so surprised she could hardly believe I was there. She looked pale and thin. The dullness of her dark eyes lit up immediately when she recognized me. Impulsively, she ran to the table where I sat and kissed me on the cheek.

"What are you doing?" screamed her uniformed escort. "That is against the rules for you to touch a visitor. Sit down across from her!"

Mama obeyed like a model prisoner.

While waiting for her, I had forgotten about the rip across the front of my blouse. The room was stuffy so I had taken off my coat. Mama spotted the rip. "What has happened to you, Lida?" The torn dress seemed to cause her more concern than her own situation.

I explained what happened on the train. Then I told her everything that was happening at home, beginning with baby Pavel, and brought her up to date on each of the children. Mama sat across from me, peace slowly filling her tired and lined face.

The two hours passed quickly. I prepared to say goodbye when the escort said, "You may come back tomorrow."

I could hardly believe it. "Oh, thank you—"

"You may have a regular family visit with her. Three days."

They made me leave then and told me to return by 9:00 the next morning. I had to walk back into the town and find a place to spend the night. I returned before nine the next morning. A guard took me to a room that measured approximately 10 feet x 7 feet. It contained two cots and a nightstand. It had one small window. Down the hallway I saw the common kitchen where we could take our food and prepare it. I had brought as much as I could carry and Mama ate heartily. She did not complain about the camp food, but I suspected she did not get enough to eat at the camp.

On the morning of the fourth day, it was a sorrowful parting for both of us. We had talked so much during the time together. We grew close during that time and we related more like two sisters than a mother and daughter.

She worried about my traveling alone going back home. "I'll be very careful this time." I also promised that I would never make the trip alone again.

Instead of going directly back to Chernogorsk, I developed a plan. I went eastward on the Trans-Siberian railway to Kansk where they had taken my sisters. I couldn't stand the thought of them staying at the *internat* any longer. Before I left the station, I bought one ticket—for Luba.

It had turned bitterly cold that morning and I had to walk quite a distance to the *internat*. I had no boots with me and my feet ached from the cold. Tears stung my face bcause my feet ached from the frigid weather. I hurt so much I felt as if I walked on stumps and each step caused excruciating pain. "I am going to make it," I repeated to myself, "if I have to crawl the last hundred feet."

I reached the building and went inside. It was about twice as large as the one where we had lived at Achinsk. I sat down on the window sill at the end of a hallway to warm my feet by propping them against the radiator. In a few minutes, a young girl, perhaps eight years old, walked down the hallway. I called to her, "There is a certain girl here named Luba Vashchenko." I tried to sound like a person of authority.

"I know her," the student said.

"Send her to me. At once."

She hurried off to find my sister Luba who would be sixteen in a few days—the normal date of release from the *internat*. We had no indication whether they would release her. I suspected that, because of our religious beliefs, they would not.

Minutes later, Luba came down the hall, unaware of who wanted her. I held up my hand to caution her. She came up close and we talked in quiet whispers as we worked out the rest of the plan. Luba left me and went to a teacher. "My sister has come to visit me from Siberia and we are going to the public baths together."

The teacher dismissed her and we went happily away from the building. As Russians know, three hours is not an unheard of length of time to wait for the baths during the daylight hours.

We had already decided that we would be foolish to go immediately home to Chernogorsk. "But we are going to leave here, together. Today."

Luba, anxious to leave, was naturally afraid but I persuaded her. "We'll not go home. First, we'll spend time with Father in prison. Surely, no one will look for us there."

She smiled and I saw the fear vanish.

We continued going east by train to visit Father who was serving the rest of his sentence in a labor camp near Reshoty. We arrived on December 27, 1968, on Luba's sixteenth birthday.

Although we were glad to see Father, I sensed something different about him but I said nothing. He sounded different, less certain of himself. Yet, the few hours we spent with him lifted our spirits and his, too, I think.

Once we returned home, we received letters from Mama. She did not complain, but I knew her heart was breaking because she was away from all of us. In the spring of 1969, I decided to visit her again.

I still had a job at the coal mine and my bosses did not want me to take time off. They said, "You are not strong, Lida Vashchenko. A trip like that will be hard on you."

"But my mother is all alone in the labor camp," I explained. "She needs someone. I must have time to go to visit her."

"No. It is a long trip. You are too young. You cannot leave your job."

They did not want me to be with Mother and to be of comfort to her. We knew that part of the government's plan was to make her worry about the family and to question whether we thought of her.

I decided to go anyway. I had already obtained permission from the labor camp to spend three days with her. I wanted time to be with her and to encourage her.

Grandmother and Grandfather, now elderly, did not want me to go. From the time I first spoke of going, Grandmother reminded me, "Remember what happened the other time? What might happen to you now?"

"Grandmother," I reminded her, "I must go to visit Mama because she needs me. You believe in prayer so you must pray for my protection." That finally stopped her and she commended me to God's safekeeping when I left.

A woman traveling alone can often get into trouble and some men consider her fair game. I had decided to take baby Pavel with me. No one would trouble a woman with a baby.

Luba packed me a parcel of food to take, enough so that Pavel and I could eat both ways on the train and also have plenty to share with Mama.

I had to stand in line to buy the ticket. I placed Pavel on the floor to one side. Next to him lay our luggage and the food. "Stay there," I told him. He seemed content to sit and watch those walking by.

As with all lines in Russia, it took time to get to the front. During the long wait, I constantly glanced around to see that Pavel was all right. Once I reached the place to buy tickets, I had my attention diverted for perhaps two full minutes. I paid for the ticket and turned around. Pavel was gone. A moment of panic set in and I ran toward my luggage. Then I saw him. He was chasing a flock of pigeons that had flown inside. They moved from spot to spot. Suddenly, they flew off toward the platform to search for crumbs and garbage at the very edge. Young Pavel went right after them.

In another few seconds he would be right at the edge of the platform. Fear clutched at my throat and I could not yell but I raced after him. The pigeons dropped down to the rails and pecked at the ground. Just then I heard an electric train coming. I never ran faster in my life. Just as Pavel reached the edge of the platform, I swooped him up into my arms and turned around. I stood there with him clutched to my breast, my breath coming in quick gasps while the train roared past.

Pavel started crying and tried to get out of my arms. He was angry because I would not let him chase the pretty birds. I hushed him the best I could and tried to keep him entertained until our train arrived.

After an uneventful trip, we arrived at Mozhaisk. Pavel was asleep in my arms when the train pulled in. Somebody kindly helped me off the train with my belongings. I arranged to leave the food and suitcase at the station, saying I would come back for them.

At the camp, I did not have to wait long this time. The escort-guard took me to Mama. As soon as she saw baby Pavel in my arms, the heaviness of her heart vanished.

She beamed so that she looked almost angelic. "Let me hold him, let me hold him," she pleaded.

Carefully she took him. I explained about having to go back to the station. She did not mind. She sat down on one of the two straight chairs in the room and gently rocked Pavel as she smoothed his rumpled hair.

When I returned, he had awakened and was sitting on Mama's lap. The instant he saw me, he jumped down and ran to me.

"Lida! Lida!" His hands were in the air, begging me to pick him up.

Mama's eyes filled with tears. My heart hurt with hers but I understood. She had been gone so long and I had taken care of Pavel most of the time since then. He had either forgotten her or felt strange around her.

"You must help him know you again, Mama," I said.

The first day was hard on both of us because of Pavel. Every time I moved, he grabbed the bottom of my skirt and followed me. I kept telling Mama that we were in a strange place and he sensed the strangeness of it.

By the second day, he would go to Mama when she called him. Before we left, he was kissing her and hugging her as he had before, calling her Mama. She felt better having her baby there and being able to spend those three days with him.

At the labor camp, they had a nursery for the children of the prisoners. Usually, all children under two years of age went to prison with their mothers. Not only did they receive poor treatment but the government sometimes allowed people to adopt the children without the mothers' consent. At least twice, camp officials urged Mama to let Pavel stay there.

That was a terrible decision for her to make. She loved that baby and he could be near her, even though she would see him only at regulated times. Her greater concern was that they would take Pavel away from her and educate him as an orphan while she was in the prison camp. Once they got him, she might not get him back.

"No, Lida, he does not belong here," she said.

In all my growing up years with Mama, I can't remember when I saw deeper pain on her face.

I nodded. I loved my brother and I would gladly take him back but I wanted it to be her choice.

"I know it is difficult for you to raise the little one and the others, too," she said and I heard the cracking of her voice. "You can leave him here if you want, but I think conditions are better at home."

"Of course I'll take him back. He'll be ready for his Mama when you get out of this terrible camp."

I had loved being with Mama but it was so hard on her. That trip also made me realize how much our family had been torn apart. Yet as I traveled back home, I was already putting the sad experiences behind me. In our family we learned to put our sorrows behind us quickly. That is the only way we have been able to continue going forward. We learned that a small happiness that lasts only minutes can brighten many days of hardship. Difficulties come but they also leave. We had three days of joy, followed by moments of pain as we parted. It was good to have the joy and that is what I wanted to remember.

Pavel rested in my arms when the train pulled out of Mozhaisk. I rocked him gently as I sang to him the hymns of our faith. How well we Vashchenkos had learned to receive comfort during times of pain and sorrow by choosing to remember the small happinesses.

NINE

The Lighter Moments

SORROW PASSED QUICKLY in our home. When happy events came, they wiped out the sad memories that preceded them. In December 1969, one year after Luba and I had visited him, we had one of our most joyous moments: Father came home.

To have him back with us again made our life seem as if he had never left us. We didn't spend a lot of time thinking about the time he had been away because we wanted to wipe away those memories. We found too much pleasure in his being with us. Had Mama been home, our happiness would have been complete.

Each day our family gathered in prayer, asking God to intervene and to release Mama soon.

In January, Father obtained a three-day permit to visit Mama at the prison camp. They worked Mama and the other women very hard, and the three-day visits also provided a chance for her to rest from the heavy work.

Three months after Father's visit, Mama wrote to the Presidium in Moscow and enclosed a medical statement that she was pregnant. On the eighth month of her pregnancy they released her. The following month she gave birth to Sarra, the twelfth child.

Even with a large family, each child brings a new kind of joy. This was true of Sarra as well as the others. Despite all the problems going on around us, we still had our family. We had peace in our own hearts. We worshiped God, even though we had to fight for that right almost every day.

We learned that, in the midst of problems and sometimes danger, life could have its lighter moments, too.

The summer following Mama's release, Vera had a chance to take a vacation by visiting with friends for a week. They lived quite a distance away so she decided to fly. Since she had to purchase her ticket in advance, I went to the airport with her.

It was such a beautiful day and the line always took a long time. "I'll sit outside and enjoy the sun while I wait for you," I said. I didn't even go inside the terminal with her.

At every airport, train station, and bus depot in Russia, the government posts KGB people in civilian clothing to watch travelers. At every ticket counter, the sellers have a book handy that contains the names and photographs of everyone the government considers troublemakers. The Vashchenkos appeared on that list.

Inside, Vera finally reached the ticket counter. She showed her identity card and travel permit as she asked for a ticket. The cashier checked her name, and immediately KGB people received a signal from the cashier to keep an eye on her. The man behind the counter kept her standing there until he was certain the KGB people had taken notice of her.

Outside I sat in the sun, enjoying the day, totally unaware of what had taken place. I could see Vera from the bench where I waited. Soon a nice-looking man about my age came out of the building. He smiled and sat down on the bench next to me. He was eating from a bag of peanuts. He smiled and offered me some.

"Thank you," I said and took a few. I munched on the nuts and said casually, "What are you doing at the airport?"

He smiled and nodded at Vera. "See that girl? The young one at the front of the line?"

"The one in the blue dress?"

"That one. I am watching her."

He did not need to say more. I knew he was telling me that he worked for the KGB. We chatted a few more minutes and then he asked, "Where do you work?"

"I work at the main KGB office."

"Ah! Then we are colleagues!" His smile broadened and he moved a little closer. "I also work for the KGB!"

"You don't mean that?"

"Oh, but I do! For eight months now." After we chatted still more, he asked, "Why are you here today instead of at the office?"

"I am also watching that girl in the blue dress."

A surprise showed on his face but before he had a chance to say anything more, Vera came outside. She read over the ticket as she walked over to the bench and sat down beside me. "The man was so slow," she said. "I wondered if he knew what he was doing."

As Vera talked idly about the ticket seller, the young man stared at me, clearly confused. Almost immediately an older man came out of the building and motioned for him to come over. He jumped up and hurried off. They talked in voices too low for us to hear. From their gestures I could see that the younger was telling the other that I was a KGB person.

The old man shook his head and grew angry. From the look on his face and the gestures he made, I could see that the young man was in trouble. I told Vera what happened and we giggled and continued to watch until the young man bowed his head and walked away in obvious disgrace, having "blown his cover."

That afternoon Vera flew off to visit her friends. I now tell people, "That was the day when I resigned from the KGB."

In 1975, my parents and five of us children traveled to Moscow on the train. Father wanted to get the forms from the American Embassy for us to immigrate to the United States. Through the kindness of Americans, we had a sponsor for our family. The difficulty lay in getting to the American Embassy without being stopped by the KGB.

The KGB was watching us closely but we did not realize that. Our train arrived in Moscow in the morning and my parents and the other children decided to go to the restrooms. They had to go down a flight of stairs and into the basement. As soon as the others headed down, I saw KGB men and policemen. Since I sat alone, they did not notice that I had not gone with the others. I could hear the officials talking to each other by radio. They decided they would close the doors to prevent their coming out. Then they would ask people to show their travel papers. Those who did not have such papers would be under arrest, and they knew we did not have such papers. "It will look like an accident," I heard one of them say. "The Americans will not realize that we were after the Vashchenkos all along."

My brother Alexander had delayed going down with them and he was the last one heading down the stairs. I called his name and ran over to him. Hurriedly I explained the KGB's plan. Ordinarily, it takes a long time to get down the narrow stairway; people are going down while others are trying to come up, and it all moves very slowly.

Alexander managed to brush past people. He got to the others, already waiting in line, and told them to go back up the steps, which they did. The KGB, caught by surprise, did not expect them to return quickly. They had not yet positioned their people.

We met in front of the station and rushed over to take the underground train. This gave us time to get across town and to complete the five-minute walk to the American Embassy. Because the guards had no warning, Father got inside, explained what he wanted, and obtained the papers that would help us start the emigration process.

The Soviet government undoubtedly knew that Father had gone inside the American Embassy and come back out again. Spies within the Embassy probably informed them of what had taken place. We knew that they would want to stop us so they could take away the papers. If we never filled out the proper forms, the government could say they did nothing to hinder our request to emigrate because they had received no such request.

To our surprise, no one stopped us as we boarded the train to return to Siberia. However, because we knew how they operated, we fully expected that upon our arrival at Chernogorsk, the authorities would be waiting for us. They would search us and, if they discovered the documents we carried, would confiscate them.

Father had been thinking about this and hit upon the only solution he thought might work. Father gave John the documents. We would all get off the train when it stopped at the next city. To confuse the one or two agents who would be watching, we would scatter, and each would walk in a different direction and mingle in the station. Father instructed John that as soon as he was sure no one followed him, he was to leave the train station and spend the night with friends in that city. The six of us would one by one return to the train and get back on for the rest of the trip home. The following day John could travel by himself the rest of the way.

That worked out all right except we still had one problem. Seven of us had boarded at Moscow and only six would arrive at Chernogorsk. How would we account for that if they asked?

"We must worry about that when it happens," Father said.

"God will help us," one of my younger sisters said.

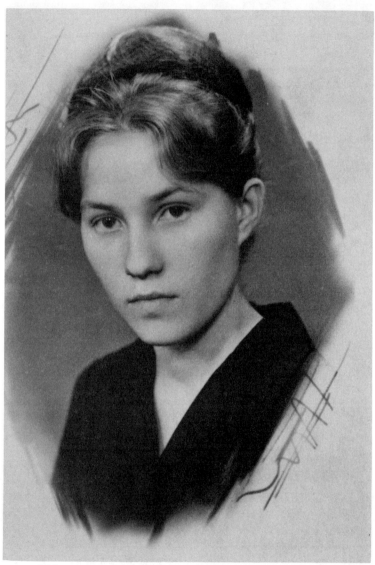

Lida

1961 First row from left: Vierra, Lila, Nadia, Luba, three cousins.
Second row from left: Lida, Sasha, grandparents, cousin.
Third row from left: Mother, John, Father, uncle, aunt, cousin.

1968 First row from left: Luba, Able, Lida, Paul, John.
Second row from left: Alexander, Lila, Jacob, Dina.

Our home in Russia with our American flag flying in the background.

The K.G.B. who came to take down the American flag outside our home.

At the hospital in Moscow after the hunger strike. Dr. Shadler from the American Embassy came to visit me every day.

A view from our room during our first month in the American Embassy in Moscow; outside in the car, the K.G.B. wait for us to leave.

In the American Embassy in Moscow.
First row from left: Lida, Lila.
Second row from left: Luba, Mother, Father.

The family at my father's funeral in Washington, D.C.

My husband, George, and I on our wedding day, August 2, 1986, Anaheim, California.

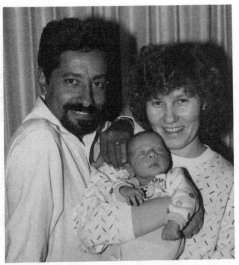

George and I with our son Jerimiah. February, 1987.

We went back to our compartment chilled and tired. Since my childhood days of running away from school, I seemed always to be sensitive to cold weather. I decided to lie down and rest. My parents covered me with their coats. That was better but my feet still felt as if they had frozen.

"We can take care of that," Father said with a hearty laugh. He took off his own fur hat and put it on my feet. These hats have straps to cover the ears, so he tied the straps around my feet to keep the hat from falling off. Within minutes my feet warmed up and I must have fallen into a deep sleep.

In the middle of the night, the compartment door opened and two security men came into the room. Though everyone else was asleep, their noise awakened me. One of them pointed the light from person to person and counted. I watched through half-closed eyes, wondering what would happen when they came up one short.

"Five, six, seven. They are all here," one of them said.

"Count again to be certain."

Now fully alert I watched as he aimed his light from face to face. Then I saw how he made the total come to seven. He counted me as one, then moved on to my sister who shared the bed with me. The light then moved down and encircled the fur hat on my feet. He counted that as the third person in our small bed.

As soon as they closed the door again, I lay in the dark and giggled. When daylight came, we laughed a long time as I told the others what happened. Father patted the fur hat, thanking it for performing a good service.

How right my sister had been when she said, "God will help us."

As expected, when we arrived at Chernogorsk, KGB men waited on the platform. They escorted us into a room and searched our luggage and our bodies. Naturally, when they searched us, we had nothing for them to confiscate. They did not seem to notice that one of us was missing because we had been reported all present before the train pulled in.

Another bright spot in the life of our family involves Ludmila. I first met her in 1977 when I had a job at a fabric-making company in the nearby town of Comosomol. She was younger, about the same age as my brother Sasha.

Ludmila, like most Russian girls, had gone through the school system and had been a member of the Young Communist League. But the deep sadness inside her showed on her face. When I saw her each day, my heart went out to her. I started talking to her.

"I hate being alive; I am ready to end it," she said once.

"I know how that feels," I said. "When I was still a schoolgirl, many times I wanted to die."

She stared at me. "But how can that be? You—you are one of the happiest people I know!"

I told Ludmila about my childhood experiences, and then I told her about coming home at age sixteen and reading the Bible again. "Since then, it has been different for me," I said. "And if I should die tonight, I know that God is with me."

"I have never heard this kind of talk before," she said cutting off the conversation.

A few days later, when we talked again, she brought up the subject of God. This kept on for several weeks. One day at our rest period, she saw me reading and came to sit down beside me.

"Lida, what book are you reading?"

"The Bible."

"You read it? You actually read it?"

"This is what our family studies. This is the book that gives us the strength to keep fighting on."

After a few more minutes of conversation, she said, "May I see your Bible?"

I handed it to her to examine. Then I told her that if she was serious, I would get her a Bible. She knew they were forbidden in Russia. I told her we had ways to get them, even though they were often expensive. She seemed deeply touched by my offer.

The next day I brought her a Bible. When we talked again, Ludmila said, "Lida, I have been reading the Bible. I don't understand it all, but I—I want to believe the way you do."

I felt overjoyed as we talked about Jesus Christ. I invited her to worship with us. "We are only twenty or thirty people, so we meet right now in our home."

"I do want to come."

After that she never missed any opportunity to be with us. Co-workers discovered this and spread the word through the factory. The authorities knew about the Vashchenkos and barely tolerated our fanatical family. But this was different. They told her she should not associate with us. They warned her of what might happen to her, including the loss of her job, but it did not stop Ludmila.

One Sunday, she had a deeply moving experience in our worship service. We call it being born again. Since we had few conversions in our city, this encouraged us greatly.

When our bosses heard that Ludmila not only continued to associate with Baptists but had actually become one herself, they put heavy pressure on her to give it up. She stood firm.

They separated us so that we had no contact in our work. That did not change Ludmila. She continued to seek me out, constantly asking me questions about God. Many times I did not know the answers myself and had to ask Father or Mama.

When they could not change Ludmila, the pressure fell on me. "What have you been doing to that nice Ludmila? You mix her up with religion, do you?"

"This used to be a good place to work," a foreman told me, "until you came here and ruined Ludmila's life with this business about God."

I received warnings and threats almost every day. "Why do you talk to me?" I finally said to my boss. "Did I force her into anything? She chose to do this on her own."

"But you caused her to."

"No. God caused it."

He became furious and screamed at me. "Don't ever talk about God to me again!"

"Then why is it that you keep bringing up the subject?" I said and smiled at him.

He talked to several workers in the factory and stirred them up. They decided to wait for me when I came out of the factory that evening. They decided they would beat me up as a warning not to do such a thing again.

Ludmila found out their plan from a coworker who boasted of what they were going to do to me. At the end of the workday, she hurried over to my new workplace in the factory and whispered, "Lida, today let's go out this other door."

"Why are we going out this way?"

"Just follow a few feet behind me and be quiet."

I followed even though I protested, "It's farther this way."

"Just be quiet." She took me out the side entrance. After we reached home she explained that she did that to protect me.

The next day the mob threatened Ludmila. "We will come to where you live and beat you so that you cannot work for a month!"

Another said, "We will beat that Baptist religion out of you."

When Ludmila told me, I made an instant decision. "Move in with me."

She did and we shared a room together until I became one of the Siberian Seven the following year. At that time, Ludmila and my brother Sasha took out marriage papers. When we emigrated, she would then be able to go with us as part of our family.

One of the happiest times of my life in the Soviet Union was when I finally was able to get the kind of job I had always wanted. Because I was a Christian, I was ridiculed wherever I worked and was assigned the dirty tasks no one else wanted to do. Not that I minded work, but often they demanded physical strength that I did not have.

Almost every job was a physically demanding and low-paying position. At one time I thought that if I worked hard and did a good job, my work would speak for itself. I soon learned that my religious beliefs barred the way toward betterment. Even when my immediate supervisor liked me, somewhere up the line another supervisor would prevent any raise in pay or promotion.

In March of 1975, however, I finally got the kind of job I wanted. That job, and the events that followed, made it the happiest period of my life. Unfortunately, the worst experience I have ever gone through as a Christian and as a human being came shortly after that.

TEN

My Aaron

FOR A LONG TIME I had wanted to work in the children's hospital. One day I read an ad in the newspaper and discovered that they needed an orderly at the local hospital. I hurried to apply.

A short, heavy-set woman came out of the office. She didn't seem to be too pleased about someone disturbing her. She looked me over and then said, "I am Neena Petrovna. Head nurse of the maternity ward. Let's go upstairs. I will show you around." She started toward the stairs, expecting me to follow her.

Neena Petrovna, a neat, slightly graying woman in her late forties, let me know she was strict with her department. We went to the second floor, which was the children's section. On the way she explained the layout of the hospital and some of the rules.

"The hospital consists of three major parts," she said, with noted authority in her voice. "The first floor is taken up by the legal abortion section. It is legal when it is done under three months of pregnancy. The second floor is divided into two parts, one for the babies and the other for the expectant mothers and those who already have given birth to the children. The first floor is not allowed to have any contact with the second floor and I don't want to ever catch anybody breaking that rule."

We came up to the nurse's changing room. We walked in and to my surprise she said, "Take all your clothes off and put on this white coat. Don't stand there and look at me, do what I told you."

I took off my coat and then my dress while she watched. She picked up my clothes, examined them and after seeing that my clothes were clean and ironed, she nodded with approval and said, "You finish dressing. I have to go and get some papers."

On that same day I filled out all of the needed papers for the job and worked four hours. The next day my name was hanging on the bulletin board with the other employees of the maternity ward.

Because my last name was well-known in the city, one of the cleaning ladies came up to me and asked, "Are you Vashchenko, the daughter of that Baptist who was on trial in 1962?"

"No," I answered, because that was not the trial of my father, but my uncle.

She figured out who I was, however. "It's all the same. You are one of those Baptists, aren't you?" she asked me laughingly.

"Yes, I believe in God," I answered her and tried to end the conversation, which I felt was not going to lead to anything good. After that when I worked with her, she usually told wild and cruel stories about terrible things Christians were supposed to have done. The tales upset the other listeners and increased their prejudice against people like me.

On the morning of March 31, 1975, I started my shift at 9:00 A.M. and would work until 6 P.M. I made the round of baby cribs, checking on them and changing their diapers. I came to one baby that lay on a large hospital bed separate from the others. He didn't have a band on his hand showing the name of his mother like the other babies.

On a sheet posted next to the bed, it said:

Child received from the criminal abortion section.
Sex: Boy. Born: March 31, 1975
Mother: Valia Vasileevna Goroshnekova.
Weight: 1 kg. 800 gr. Length: 32 cm.

In our building the doctors performed only legal abortions, but in another building located two blocks from us was the criminal abortion section. This was for women who went beyond three months of pregnancy before they decided to go ahead with the abortion. Some women believe it is easier on them to delay the abortion until the seventh or eighth month and then artificially induce labor. Those women usually go to a midwife or a retired doctor who induces labor. After the labor pains begin, the women call the hospital and an ambulance brings them to the criminal abortion section to finish the job.

Sometimes the job is unsuccessful—the baby comes out alive. The staff often can't decide what to do with this human being. If, after waiting for a couple of hours, the infant does not die, they bring it to the children's section of the hospital.

While I worked there, about twenty-five women came in every day to get abortions in the legal section. Of the seven or eight who entered the criminal section, three or four of them gave live birth. The aborted child usually died from neglect within a few days.

I kept looking at the little boy all by himself. Everyone expected him to die. He was so small, he almost didn't seem to be a real child. I could fit him on my hand easily. His forehead and cheeks were covered with burns, probably the result of something used in inducing labor.

As I touched him, I thought, this baby was brought into the world, not by his own desire but by the act of others. Now he is sentenced to die. Was it his fault he was born alive?

I knew what I had to do—although it meant going against everybody around me. I leaned over and touched him on his cheeks and forehead. I whispered, "You go ahead and live, little one! Let them desire your death, but you go ahead and live!"

Neena Petrovna, in the same room, turned around and saw me as I was touching him. With a threatening tone of voice she said, "Lida, don't touch him! We don't know yet what they poisoned him with. You can catch something."

Reluctantly, I walked on to another child and started to change his diapers. I went through the motions, but my mind was still thinking about that poor baby boy and the cruel way he had come into this world.

Neena continued her work but she was obviously disturbed with the baby being here. "They brought him at night. I found him in the hallway."

He was not showing strong signs of life and everybody thought he was going to die. The doctors had not yet decided what to do with him.

"The mother aborted him at seven months," Neena said, "I just can't understand something like that. It's like a murder. So what if she was not married and did not have any place to take him? She did not have to kill him because of that. Now he is alive, yet at the same time he is not."

For the first time, this woman who seemed so hard showed a streak of kindness and concern. But at the same time, she spoke out of the frustration of not being able to change this cruel reality.

At lunch time we were starting on our meal when the cleaning lady from the criminal section came in with a bundled-up infant in her arms and he was crying. Another little one lived, I thought.

"We are at lunch," one of the nurses yelled. "Stop that noise! You have to wait until we finish. We are tired anyhow."

"But he is crying and needs to be cleaned up. He stayed with us for about two hours and did not die. You have to take him now!" He was a little larger than the baby boy I had been concerned about earlier.

"No, not at lunch. Take him back and bring him later."

"But it is cold outside. He hardly has anything wrapped around on him," she insisted.

"So what? Nobody wants him anyhow," the nurse answered.

Another orderly, with whom I got along well, sat at the table next to me. She stopped eating and watched.

"Zoia," I said to her quietly, "let's take him and clean him up. We can come back to lunch later."

"Sure," she agreed, and together we took the newborn.

"Thank you so much. He is a person, even if he looks like this. I feel sorry for him," she said as she gave the baby to us.

"See our best workers. They have more pity than the others," said one of the nurses mockingly. "Hey, Zoia, maybe you are one of those Baptists?" the other nurses said laughingly.

"We will be back in a few minutes," Zoia said, as if she did not hear their comments.

"I am so thankful to you for coming with me. I am new here, so who am I to take this baby?" I said to her.

"Oh, why are you thanking me? I felt sorry for him myself. I have a one-year-old son, so every time I see one of these babies, I imagine him in this place. I also feel sorry for those mothers. Either they give birth or have an abortion. I don't want a lot of babies either, but what else is there to do?"

After cleaning him up, we put him next to the other premature infant. Two of them, side by side, neither wanted by anyone.

A week later when I came to work I saw a dead baby laying on the floor. It was the child that Zoia and I had picked up and cleaned. He had obviously died during the night. I felt such a sense of sadness for that little one who never had a chance to know life.

"Lida, take him to the boiler room in the basement," said the senior orderly who was getting off her shift.

I didn't understand right away why I had to take the poor child to the boiler room in the basement until after I got there. I carried him carefully on the way down because, even though dead, he was still a person.

As I saw children like that, the old hymn would come to my memory.

Why do flowers grow and blossom,
Those most fragile of God's creations?
For a short moment they open, and all they see,
A world full of pain and frustration.
They never murmur or cry
In a twinkling sunset of their lives.
And at this moment, in silent beauty
With holy patience they come and die.

A woman working in the boiler room took the child from me and placed him on the scoop of a shovel. She took off the scanty blankets, handed them to me, and threw the lifeless body inside. He landed on top of the red coals, which brought him into movement. His legs and his arms rose up and—it seemed to me that for a moment, he came to life. The hot burning flames of the fire danced around the body. It almost seemed that they were celebrating his death in some kind of dance ritual. Pain went through to my very heart. I began to feel terrible, as if there was not enough air in the room. Unable to stand any more, I ran from the basement.

I found it impossible to erase that scene from my mind. In the legal ward, I walked by rooms of women who had had abortions, and others who were talking happily, waiting for their turn to get one. It seemed they had no pity, their hearts did not ache during the convulsions of their babies before their babies died. I could not understand such hardness.

In the days that followed, I kept visiting that baby boy who insisted on living. I called him Aaron. I liked that name because it came from the Bible. I often stood by his bedside and stroked his face and looked at him for a long time. When he awakened I changed his grey, dirty diapers and put him into clean ones. Then I would take his small, cold body and begin warming it over the hot plate. After he warmed up a little, I would wrap him in more diapers and put him back in his crib and pack hot water bottles around him.

When I was not working nobody else changed his hot water bottles, and he would lay there for hours with cold bottles next to his tiny, shivering body. Somehow that child held on. He was living while everyone waited for his death. His mother did not want him and neither did anyone else. No one but me.

They did not keep a history of his birth or medical chart. I frequently overheard doctors and nurses discuss him when they started their shifts.

"Did the poor one die?"

"No, still living. It is strange how much he wants to live. He is just climbing out from death."

"I tell you, he should just go ahead and die so that would be the end of it. No one wants to have anything to do with him, not even his mother."

They could not understand why he was still alive because he was receiving no attention. They would even forget to change his diapers. I liked to believe that Aaron remained alive because God put love and pity for him in my heart. A baby cannot live without the caring touch of another human or without the warmth of love. I also believed that he could hear me talking and understood that at least one person cared. He would not be totally alone because somebody loved him.

An examining committee made surprise visits to the hospital to check on the children. The doctors had to account for every death. If the evidence showed a death was their fault, they could lose their quarterly or even yearly bonuses. Consequently, they let the aborted babies die without reporting them, making it look as if they never lived. Aborted (although living) babies were not counted as living because they always died—all but little Aaron.

As I kept taking care of poor Aaron, I remembered my own childhood life in the orphanage when I was separated from my parents. I felt there was a common bond between us. I wanted to help him so much. One day I thought, maybe I can talk to Mikhail about it. Why can't I, at twenty-four, replace his mother?

Mikhail and I had met in church and developed a deep friendship. We did not understand dating and romance as people of the Western world do, so it is difficult to explain our relationship other than to say we expected to marry.

Mikhail usually walked me to work and one morning I finally decided to tell him about the baby, hoping that he would feel about it as I did. I told him everything and ended with, "I want that baby."

"We will have babies of our own. We will have a lot of babies after we get married."

"No, I want to adopt that baby I call Aaron. He wants to live. He is strong. Mikhail, he really needs me."

"This is something new. You're quite serious about this, aren't you?" He did not seem to know what to say or how to react to this kind of news.

"Oh, yes, and if you could see him, I know you would understand." I hurried on with my ideas. "We could register our marriage now and adopt him right away."

Mikhail's big green eyes were still staring at me, not fully comprehending my excitement.

I decided he needed a little more convincing. "Come into the hospital with me, Mikhail; I can show you the baby."

He agreed. When we got there, I rushed upstairs and brought the little boy down. Fortunately, no one was around because I was breaking the rules of the hospital. I loved that baby so much that, at the moment, I didn't care. Aaron was sleeping and looked so peaceful.

"He is a precious, tiny person," I said. "God knows I want to help him so much." I was going on about the baby, and Mikhail stood there looking at both of us. He didn't seem to know how to take this new addition to his future family.

"I must go," he finally said. "I'll think about it. I will see you in a couple of days." He opened the door, stood there a moment and stared once more at me with the child in my arms. Then he turned and left.

I slowly walked upstairs trying not to wake the baby. I watched his little mouth moving almost as if he were trying to say something through his sleep. "Don't worry, Aaron, I won't leave you. I don't know what Mikhail is going to do but I know what I am going to do."

A few days later Mikhail and I talked again. I could see that he had something on his mind. He was trying to smile as he talked, but he was not very natural. We walked out of the house and strolled down the street.

"You know, Lida, you almost convinced me to be a father to the baby," he said. "You can talk with such pretty words. You make it all sound so good that you move me to pity. I have talked to my parents about it, and I want to hold to their advice. They don't think I should get involved in something like this right now."

"Your parents?" I asked. "But how do you feel?"

"But, Lida, they would not wish me anything bad, would they?"

"Of course not," I replied, "but God teaches us to solve questions like this ourselves. We have to decide if we want to help this poor creature who was denied by his own mother. How can you listen to someone else's advice on a subject like this? You have to decide for yourself if you want to help."

"It's not so easy to—to make such decisions."

"In my life, I decide everything by myself. Since I was eleven years old, I have been on my own without parents. It is easy for me to make up my mind."

I realize now that my love for that child outweighed everything. I was not kind to Mikhail because I could think only of the child no one else wanted. We talked a long time. Finally, I asked, "Will you come to the registry office to help me or not?"

"I don't know. My father told me that we will be visiting Berlin to celebrate the New Year," he said. (Mikhail is of German descent and for years the family had been trying to emigrate to Germany.) "You are Russian and you want to have this baby. If I marry you now with the adopted child, we might never be able to emigrate with the whole family. That is what my parents fear. So I don't know what to do."

"I find it strange that a grown man can't make up his mind at an important time like this. I look at life as the Bible teaches us to, as God has spoken to us. Here is a life we can save—you and I. Is emigration more important than a child's life?"

I didn't give him a chance to argue and said abruptly, "It is useless for us to continue this conversation. I'll be at the registry office tomorrow. You do as you wish!"

I was not kind to Mikhail, but I could think of little except that infant. If I did not adopt him, I had no question about his future. He would die from neglect.

"I can feel how strongly you care—but—but we'll see," he said.

"Sure, we will see, but maybe it will be too late. I need to have your last name for the baby because everybody knows the name Vashchenko well, and it would be very dangerous for Aaron. The government might refuse to register him to me. Can you understand how important this is? We can register our marriage and adopt Aaron, and then a month later, if you like, I will bring you all of the documents for a divorce. You will not be responsible for him in the future. Or, if your family does not receive their emigration papers and mine does, you could come with me as my husband, just for helping to save the baby. Then as soon as we are over the border, you will be free from this marriage. We can do it either way."

"That's an interesting plan," he said and I saw the spark of interest in his eyes. "But is your family really going to emigrate? I am not very sure about that. After all, with the trouble your family has had—"

"But I am sure, and believe me, I will do anything to help you, if you help me now. Can you understand how precious this baby is to me?"

"Maybe I can come tomorrow," he said slowly.

We parted and I went to work. After taking over my shift I went to see Aaron. I stood there looking at his little helpless body. He was sleeping and didn't know that at that very moment his whole future was in the balance. Only that morning Mama had said realistically, "Lida, I think your efforts are wasted. The government will not give him to you." Although I knew she was probably right, I could not give up and abandon Aaron. I decided not to say anything more to the family until I got all of the documents for the baby's adoption.

I decided to talk to Valia, Aaron's mother. I kept arguing with myself as I went to where she lived, "Maybe she will not listen to me. No, she won't. Yes, she will because she does not want the baby. She will give him to me!"

I felt so close to Aaron, as if he were already mine. To meet with his mother terrified me, but my love for him drove me forward.

I had learned that she lived in an *obscheiutee,* a place for people without apartments of their own. Because of the shortage of living space, the government supplies these boarding houses for the unfortunate ones.

The hostel were Valia lived was for people with children and families only. It had two stories and about two hundred rooms, each about 10 feet x 12 feet. Each floor had a toilet and a sink that was used by all the tenants on the floor. The building had two wings, each with its own kitchen. Each kitchen contained a couple of stoves, some kitchen tables, and a refrigerator that was used only by tenants who wanted their food to be stolen. There were also showers for men and women downstairs, if they wished to use them. Such quarters provided a lot of closeness and plenty of unwanted fellowship.

Many boarders were at work during the day. Strollers were standing next to some of the doors, and I could hear babies crying. Some of them were probably born without fathers. But they were lucky. At least their mothers did not deny them.

When I located her, I said, "Hello, Valia. I am from the maternity hospital." It seemed as if a shadow crossed Valia's face. "Can I talk to you, please?"

"Yes," she said, but there was suspicion in her voice. She let me inside. "The room isn't mine, it belongs to a friend. I am staying with her temporarily."

I explained why I had come. "So I want to adopt him if it is okay with you."

I heard her taking a sigh of relief, and a smile appeared on her small, thin face for the first time since we had met. She was a tall, beautifully built woman, with delicate features and big brown eyes.

"You can adopt him. I was frightened because I thought you came to find me and force me to take him back, and I don't know what to do with him. I don't have a place to live or any clothes for him. I am so unlucky! Everybody has abortions and it ends well, but for me—" She started to cry.

I took her by the hand and said, "Don't cry. I will take him and I believe that he will grow up to be a good person."

She looked at me with disbelief. Then, as if she just woke up, she said, "I want to show you a picture of his father." She reached for a portrait and handed it to me. Looking at me from the picture was a handsome, tall young man.

"He is now in the army," she explained, "but I want to marry someone else. That is why I don't want this baby."

"Does he know that he has a son?" I asked wondering about the man.

She shook her head. "He asked me to go ahead and have the baby and he would come back from the army and marry me. I told him I wouldn't. He doesn't know I waited this long with the abortion."

"I need a piece of paper saying that you agree to let me adopt the baby. I won't tell anyone about it. You can keep the money that is due to you at work for maternity leave before and after birth. I don't need anything."

It seemed strange to her to meet somebody who wanted her aborted baby and who was willing to give her the money that didn't belong to her anymore. She needed this money. At the same time, it was hard not to notice joy and hope in her eyes. "Is it possible that all of this will end so well?"

She signed the following statement:

I, Goroshnekova Valia V. renounce the rights over my child born on March 31, 1975. In the future I will not make any demands about him.

At the hospital's administrative office, in exchange for her statement, I was given the birth documents for the baby. The documents stated that the child was mine.

The last step would involve going to the registry office the next morning. I hoped Mikhail would meet me there. Yet I knew God would make everything work out fine, no matter what Mikhail decided.

I told my family everything that night. The news upset the family, especially Mama. She knew, better than anyone, the problems I would face in taking this step. Although she spoke out of concern for me, I could think only of that infant, lying alone in a hospital and needing my love.

As I continued to talk, I think she realized my determination. She finally said, "Do what seems best to you."

"That is what I needed to hear," I told her.

The next morning, I stood in front of the building waiting for Mikhail. I stayed a full hour. Every few minutes, I whispered to myself, "He will be here any minute. We will register our marriage and then register the baby under his name." Yet, in my heart, I didn't know.

I hoped to see him walking toward me, and yet at the same time a sinking feeling inside told me that I would be disappointed. It saddened my heart to think that after a friendship of two years, he would fail me in this time of trial.

Mikhail never came to the registry office.

My heart was racing when I came near the registry office. The workers there knew me well and knew the convictions of my family. However, that morning a new girl was in charge of registering newborns and deaths. She was quite young and did not seem confident of what she was doing. It took her a long time to write everything in the book. After that she slowly filled out the certificate and said to me, "I have to get it signed by our supervisor. Wait here just a minute." She disappeared through the door of the office opposite her. I could hear voices coming through the door.

Vera Vaseleevna, the supervisor, came out of the office to see me. "Hello, Lida Vashchenko," and with a smile she handed me the certificate.

"Hello, Vera Vaseleevna," I answered, fearing that she knew everything.

"So you gave him birth?" She was looking me up and down with contempt in her eyes. "Where is your husband?"

"I have no husband."

"Oh! Vashchenko girls are now having babies without husbands!" She smiled again as she said it, "Yes, we all are sinners, aren't we? But that is all right. You can raise him, can't you?"

"Of course I can," I said, beginning to realize there might be hope.

"Why do you call him Aaron?"

"It is a name from the Bible and I like it."

"From the Bible? Without a husband and from the Bible?" she laughed, "Oh, girl, girl, I feel sorry for you. Soon you will understand that there is no God!" She laughed again and told the clerk about me, making several unkind remarks for my benefit.

She walked away, going back to her office. Then she did a strange thing. She turned and said in a kind voice, "Good luck to you in bringing up the little one."

After leaving the registry office, I hurried back to the hospital. The baby now had my name, and I had a right to take him home!

Aaron was mine. My son.

Regardless of the terrible events that happened later, nothing will ever ruin that moment of pure happiness for me.

ELEVEN

From My Arms

A DOPTING AARON SEEMED SIMPLE compared to the problems that faced me later.

I decided to live at the hospital with Aaron, so I could watch over him and see with my own eyes what kind of treatment he was getting. Right away I could see that the care he was receiving was terrible. He had not been washed since he was transferred to the children's section. The other mothers with sick children hardly ever came up to him. When he cried, nobody cared enough to find out what was wrong. The mothers were afraid that the sickness he had would spread to their children. Because he looked so bad, they were not sure how contagious the sickness was.

None of the staff people liked the idea of my adopting Aaron, and they showed it in the way they treated me and neglected him.

Aaron had been born sick and weak, yet he was getting better. He would have gotten better much faster if he had received proper care when I was not around. If I was not there to watch, they passed him by when they cared for the other infants.

Even though I fought the idea for a long time, I soon realized that the only chance for Aaron's survival was to take him out of the hospital. Although he was mine legally, they would not release him.

Once I accepted the situation as it was, I decided the next step was to kidnap my own son. After all of the experiences of growing up in the Vashchenko family, I had become an expert in doing things like this.

I waited until 10:00 P.M. on the night of May 10, 1975. The doctors and nurses had finished making their last rounds and checking on the patients. I went into the nursery and wrapped Aaron in a warm blanket and then covered him with a newspaper so that he looked like nothing more than a package of dirty clothes I was taking home with me.

I made a little hole in the newspaper so he would not suffocate. I paused and said under my breath, "Help me, God." Then I boldly walked to the door and out of the room. Many thoughts raced through my mind, but one was stronger than the others. "If only they don't notice me."

The nurse at the door leading to the stairs was dozing off with her head in her arms on the table. The light in the hallway was dim. I did not have the time to wait until Aaron was fully asleep because if I would let the time slip by and not go right away, it could be too late. On the stairs he made fussing sounds, letting me know he was not satisfied with his position. I clutched him tighter, hoping to overcome his sounds of dissatisfaction with the rustle of the paper.

We went into my room. I took the warm blanket from my bed and bundled him up inside it. I climbed up to the window sill. The window opened with some difficulty. After putting on my raincoat, I picked up the child and listened for the last time for any noise coming from the hallway. After being assured there was nobody coming in our direction and that the courtyard was empty, I jumped out of the window.

Without doubt, the authorities would come looking for me and Aaron. They did not care about me or about the baby. But because, as a Vashchenko, we had challenged the Soviet system so many times, they would not let us get away with anything.

Within three days, doctors came to the house and wanted to take Aaron back to the hospital for additional treatment. I refused.

I knew that would not end the problem and that they would return. That night, to avert the watching eyes of the KGB, I dressed up like a boy, put Aaron in a small barrel where I kept him well covered, and rode in a horse-drawn cart to the countryside. I stayed with Christian friends.

I remained there for several weeks until I was sure the authorities had stopped troubling my family. Then, once again, I dressed up as a boy. This time I borrowed a bicycle, and with Aaron strapped to me, I rode home to Chernogorsk.

It did not take long before the police put our house under surveillance. Someone had reported my return, obviously.

A few days later, my sister Sarra (then age five) went with me while I pushed the baby in a carriage. We came home the back way just in time to see a police car pull up. We hid until they left. The incident told me that they would not stop coming.

Maria Chmykhalov, who had been a member of the church since about 1954, kindly took me and baby Aaron in. This put them in a great deal of danger if they were caught. Others who might have helped turned their backs on me because they were afraid.

I remember one night in her home, I was praying and thanking God for the Chmykhalov family and I said, "God, I wish I could do something for them, to repay them in some way for their help."

I had no way of knowing that circumstances would come about years later when I would be faced with the answer to that prayer—and at a time when I would not be inclined to help.

When I first took Aaron and showed him attention, he wanted it every second. When he started to cry and no one came immediately, he picked up a little trick. He stopped crying and held his breath until he turned pale. He would hold it as long as he could and then exhale. The crying started again. If no one came immediately, he repeated the process.

I tried to give him as much love and attention as possible. When he started to cry, I did not always pick him up. Sometimes I only touched him lightly. Always I talked softly to him. Even from across the room if I spoke softly to him, that seemed to reassure him. The breath holding became less frequent.

Then the inevitable happened. On July 17, 1975, we heard a knock on the door. Outside stood a woman we knew well, Lila Dugina, Instructor on Religious Affairs, along with Rimma Alekseevna, a member of the executive committee of the communist party in Chernogorsk. A third woman stood a little behind them and it took me a few seconds to recognize her as Aaron's natural mother, Valia.

Although they demanded to come inside, we refused to let them.

Dugina did most of the talking. She finally yelled, "This poor mother stands out here, broken-hearted, aching for the son you have stolen from her."

Rimma Alekseevna added, "Have you no conscience? Would you deny this poor mother the chance to see her son? She is blinded by her grief!"

Vera called back, "Look at the mother! She doesn't look broken-hearted to us! Where was her bleeding heart when she aborted him? Where were the tears when she refused to nurse him and left him behind at the hospital?"

Of course, they couldn't win by arguing. Instead they demanded more strongly that we let them inside. I don't remember how long they argued but soon a car, filled with uniformed men, pulled up. One of them, a police investigator, grabbed the fencegate and shook it. "Unlock this immediately! Open the gate!"

Behind him another man held up several sheets of paper. "We have official documents. We represent the Soviet government! You must let us inside at once!"

Neighbors began to gather to watch the scene. One of them explained to the rest of the crowd that the authorities had come to recover the baby that the Vashchenkos had stolen.

Another one yelled, "We have come to stop them before they sacrifice the child!" (In the Soviet Union, many atheists have been led to believe that Christians sacrifice children. They point out the story in Genesis 22 where Abraham prepared to offer his son Isaac as a sacrifice.)

Vera courageously battled them with words. Usually, I was the one to do that, but not this time. I could do nothing but clutch my son. He was asleep during this terrible time and I was glad I did not have to soothe him.

I heard the voice of a woman neighbor, "This is how you Christians do things. You find a person in misfortune and act as if you want to help. You followed Valia in her grief and bought her child when she was half out of her mind!"

Finally, one of the policemen took the large window pane out of the window. They pushed Valia (the birth mother) to the window so that I could see her.

"Tell her," the man prompted.

"You are a scoundrel!" she said.

Even though I knew she had been forced to come, I stood up to her. "Why do you call me that? You know better."

"Because—because you did a mean thing."

"What did I do?"

For a few seconds she did not know how to answer. Finally, a few halting words came out. "I—I did not know you were that kind of person."

"Valia, what kind of person?"

I felt sorry for her. She did not want the baby and yet she feared the people who were with her. She stood in silence and finally blurted out, "Give me my baby."

"Valia, you don't want him. What is he to you?"

She dropped her head, no longer able to look at me. Someone nudged her several times but she did nothing. Then she received a heavy push so that she almost fell against the window. She turned around and I heard voices whispering and giving instructions. Valia faced me again, not looking at me. "Give him up. I need him."

"When did you start to need him?"

She could no longer participate in it. She shook her head and turned away. Behind her, voices demanded that she climb inside and take the child away from me.

"You cannot do this!" I screamed from across the room. "If you come inside, you are committing an illegal act." With my free hand, I grabbed a walking cane. "Valia, I will beat you with this if you try to enter."

She tried to turn away but someone stopped her. "Please—please" she said to them. She started to cry because she did not want the child, and I knew she did not want to cause me any trouble. A policeman took her arm until she calmed down.

Minutes later a small-sized policeman, brandishing a gun, jumped at the window and crawled through. The next thing I knew two other policemen were in the room. One of them bent my free arm behind me and a second one pulled me by the hair. They slung me to the sofa. I still had Aaron in my arms and one of them grabbed him from me.

Aaron woke up then and started to cry. I did not know what to do to soothe him. I stared in helplessness as he held his breath.

"Wait! I won't do anything!" I bent over and kissed him on the cheek. "Aaron, my sweet one." He began to breathe normally.

The man pulled Aaron away and carrying him upside down, he handed the baby out to Valia. The policeman standing next to her ordered, "Take it."

"Aaron!" I lurched toward the window.

The policeman with the gun pushed me away from the window. I staggered and fell against the sofa. I think I passed out because I don't remember seeing them leave. I did hear the car door slam and the sound of the car engines starting.

I could do nothing but weep without stopping. They had taken him. I had no idea if I would ever see him again. I could not stop crying for hours.

We later heard that Valia, the birth mother, had refused to take Aaron. However, she did get a nice apartment to rent because of her cooperation. Along with this, a rumor spread around Chernogorsk that I had beaten a policeman but that because the city authorities were humane people who realized it had been enough of a disgrace that both my parents had been imprisoned, they would generously overlook prosecuting me this time.

Naturally, I appealed to the local officials for Aaron's return, but as a mere formality. I knew they would not help me and would tell me nothing.

In desperation, on August 16, 1975, more than a month after Aaron's abduction, I wrote a letter of appeal for help to the United Nations. I told them the entire story.

The city executive committee suggested that I forget about the child and go back to work. "If I knew where my baby is, I would go to work there cleaning floors. But until I know his whereabouts, I will go nowhere."

On August 22, my father and three of the children insisted that I go into the forest with them and pick wild berries to get my mind off of Aaron. I did not want to go. What if word came while I was gone? They persuaded me to go. We had a good time picking a large quantity of berries to preserve for food during the winter months. I tried to smile and to act normal, but I could not get my thoughts away from my son.

On the evening of August 24, 1975, we returned by traveling in the open flat-bed freight car of the train. It started to rain lightly but steadily. Despite our rainslickers, eventually we got soaked as we rode along.

Then, without warning, I began to cry. I crawled over to Father and realized that he had started to cry. At least one of the other children was also crying. "I have this sense—this sense of something very wrong." I said.

It was a kind of crying I had not done before. The tears did not stop, yet I did not know why I cried. I started to pray silently. After perhaps half an hour, a sense of peace came over me and the tears stopped.

No matter what we did, we could find out nothing about the baby. In another desperate act, we decided to contact the American Embassy again. Christian friends joined Father, Mama, and me as we took the train to Moscow again. We did not have permission to travel, so we knew we might be stopped. Fortunately, none of the authorities ever challenged us. We reached Moscow, went directly to the American Embassy. To our surprise, most of us were able to walk inside. We explained about the abduction of Aaron.

They promised to help in any way they could. When we got up to leave, they gave us a document to show the policemen at the gate and a telephone number if anyone stopped us. A consular officer walked out with us and escorted us beyond the Embassy area. No one tried to stop us but KGB agents followed us, keeping at a discreet distance. By this time, we could easily recognize them, no matter how they dressed or how they tried not to be known.

Back in Chernogorsk, I again went to the office of the city committee. This time I spoke with Galina Andruishchenko, the vice-chairman of the executive committee. I kept asking questions and I finally told her about our trip to Moscow (although I suspect she already knew that). I added that the Americans were investigating, saying, "If you don't tell me, they will soon find out anyway."

"I see," she said, believing my words. "I do know where the child is but you are unable to see him right now. He is at the Abakan children's hospital."

"But surely if I go there—"

"No! He is having an expensive medical treatment and you will not be admitted."

I persisted in asking for permission to visit. I promised that I would not attempt to take the baby away.

Finally, she said, "I'll check on his condition. Come back in three days' time. If possible, I shall then arrange for you to see him."

Three days later, on September 18, 1975, I returned. This time I carried some of Aaron's clothes.

"Ah, Lida Vashchenko, how lovely you look today—"

"Please," I interrupted. "I have come about the baby. If you won't let me have him, at least allow me to see him again and give him these clothes." I held up what I had brought.

"You cannot see him."

"But you promised. Please."

"The truth is, the boy is no longer alive. He died."

"I don't believe you," I said. I didn't want to believe her.

"It is true. If you like, I can show you where he is buried."

"Yes, this you must do." Despite the deep pain in my heart, I had to be certain that Aaron had died. They could easily use this as a trick to make us stop looking for him.

From the Bureau of Technical Information where they keep a list of those who die without relatives, my father received a death certificate for Aaron. I made a copy of it.

We also talked to the coffinmaker who described the baby for whom he had made the coffin. My heart broke when he said, "It was impossible to make out what he had looked like because his body was badly decomposed. There was no nose and his eyes had disappeared."

Early the next morning we went to the cemetery about eight miles north of the city. We talked with the old woman who had worked there for many years. She told us that they had buried a baby there only three or four days earlier. "The police said they found his body in a field and that he was already starting to decompose. They did not know anything about his parents or family."

We dug up the grave, glancing around all the time to see if anyone watched. We were breaking the law. Although the body had been badly disfigured, I easily recognized my son from the forehead, the hands, and the legs.

No doubt remained about Aaron. My sweet, innocent son was dead.

As we reconstructed events, Aaron died on August 24—the very time when we were traveling on the flat-bed train when we suddenly started to weep. They had allowed his body to remain in the morgue for two and a half weeks.

At home that night we turned the radio to the Far Eastern Broadcasting network. We heard a Russian-language program that came from Korea. The special music and the message was the kind that we might have heard at a funeral. It seemed to us as if that message had come just for us at that moment and we felt a deep sense of peace.

The next day we held a Christian burial. I would have liked to invite a few Christians who knew Aaron, but it was too dangerous. I shed many tears that day but vowed that I would no longer cry for Aaron. He had been my son for five months. Those months had been the happiest times of my entire life. Aaron was now beyond pain and neglect. Never again would he know rejection or feel unloved.

As we finished the burial service, God granted me peace and the pain subsided. How deeply I needed God's peace because I knew I would never see my lovely son again in this life.

TWELVE

The Big Step

AFTER AARON'S BURIAL, I tried to go back to living as I had before. Something had happened to me that made me more determined than ever to emigrate. Before then, it had been primarily the desire of my parents, now it became an obsession with me. I could never find true happiness in this land where civil authorities had murdered my son, an infant who had never done anything wrong.

The following year, Father's mother died at the age of eighty-four. She never saw her dream of emigrating fulfilled. A few weeks later, my brother Sasha turned eighteen. Because he refused to serve in the armed forces, the state tried him and gave him a three-year sentence. They sent him to Minusinsk where Father had been imprisoned. A few months later they transferred him to a labor camp northeast of Chernogorsk. It took us eighteen hours by train to reach there.

Although we did not know it, things had already begun to change. About the time of Sasha's trial, the Reverend Cecil J. Williamson, Jr. sent us a formal *vyzov* (invitation) to America. This pastor of the Hill Presbyterian Church in Selma, Alabama, heard about Pentecostals in the Soviet Union through the Tolstoy foundation in New York. He, along with church officers, issued us a formal invitation, saying that they would sponsor our family in the United States. We did not receive the *vyzov* until April 20, 1978—four months after it was sent.

During the months after Aaron's death, we continued to suffer persecution. The authorities prepared court cases to take away the youngest children in our family. Sometimes they fined us. On other occasions they interrupted us in the middle of a worship service to insist that we were meeting illegally. It was the old pattern again. But we had committed ourselves to God and determined that they could do nothing to stop us.

By this time, I no longer feared what could happen. The state had taken from me the most precious thing in the world, other than my own life, that of Aaron. Nothing could frighten me now.

When Father received the invitation, we felt a sense of joy and deep concern. We knew that other families had received their own *vyzov,* had gone to the authorities, and had them confiscated. We would not allow them to deceive us again. But what should we do? We were tired of appealing to the immigration authorities. We had already had bad experiences by going to the American Embassy. What could we do?

My parents had tried everything to get permission to leave but nothing worked out. They tried to hand in our citizenship papers to receive exit visas, but nothing came of that. My father applied to Chernogorsk, to the territorial capital at Krasnoyarsk, and from office to office. No one ever did anything to help us.

Father and Mama said we would fast and pray; then God would give us an answer. We had one ray of hope. In 1975, when we went to the American Embassy about Aaron's disappearance, we had received a pass to show the police at the gate. As we understood from Father's conversation with the Embassy officials at that time, they would help us to emigrate to the United States if we had a sponsor. We now had one.

After two or three days of prayer and fasting, Mama, I, and some of the older children felt our only chance lay in returning once again to the American Embassy. Father disagreed.

"We have no other choice," Mama said. "We must go back. As the children are now all growing up, some of them will marry and have families. They will go their own ways. How could we possibly get them all together then?"

"I don't think we should—"

"Who else will help us?" Mama insisted.

Father argued against the plan. Mama finally declared that she would go with or without him. "I know this is right." I agreed with her.

"Then you go without me," Father answered.

It hurt me to see Father that way. I knew he was afraid of being taken back to the psychiatric hospital. They told him upon his release: "This is your last chance. If you ever come back here again, you will stay here forever." I understood his fear, but I also knew that if we did not attempt once again to gain our right to emigrate, we might never have another chance.

He also knew that if the KGB came to arrest anyone in the family, he would be first. He did not want to go back to the American Embassy. Yet he could not remain at home and continue to protest without also being in danger. It seemed that no matter what decision Father made, it would bring him more trouble.

We all knew the dangers involved, especially that it is against the law for the citizens of the Soviet Union to ask a foreign Embassy for help.

We decided to pray about it and asked, "God, show us what to do. We will vote and you show us that way." Each of us, except the youngest children, took a piece of paper. "Should we go? Yes, or no?" Father said. I could tell by the way he asked that he hoped we would vote against going.

The majority voted to go.

We finally decided that only five of us would make the trip. The KGB would be watching us carefully. We knew that we could not all make the trip because then the KGB would realize what we were doing and would never allow so many of us to go at one time. We five bought our tickets in advance and decided that we would leave in separate groups. Our plan was to reach the American Embassy and appeal for their help in securing exit visas.

We also knew that if the Americans helped us, we would not have to return to Chernogorsk. The rest of the family would be free to follow us because we would have the necessary documents.

On the evening of June 23, 1978, we left. John planned to take his motorcycle, filling the sidecar with food for the journey. At the last minute, Maria Chmykhalov and her son Timothy appealed to us to go with us. Timothy rode on the motorcycle to the station with John. The next day, Jacob would go to the place where John planned to hide the motorcycle and bring it home.

Mama and Maria planned to go out the front door, strolling along like two neighbors who wanted an evening walk. At the last minute, Father chose to join them.

My two sisters and I started out last. We went out the back door and took a different street. We tried to appear casual and playful to the neighbors sitting in front of their homes on that lovely summer evening, as though we had no destination in mind. We crossed the fields on foot and reached the main road.

We boarded the express train that went directly to Moscow. The six—including Father—in our family stayed in two groups while Maria and Timothy traveled together. The KGB had personnel on duty that did not know us. On the third day, however, the KGB identified the Chmykhalovs and kept them under surveillance. But, typical of them, they did nothing to hinder anyone. They watched, probably made extensive notes, but nothing else.

Upon arrival at Moscow, the Chmykhalovs somehow lost the KGB that followed them. We all met at the metro and took it to the American Embassy.

Now you know the circumstances and events leading up to our stay in the American Embassy in Moscow and the twenty-eight day fast that led to my being taken by car to Botkin Hospital. I did not expect to live.

Television cameras and reporters followed the car when we left the American Embassy. At the hospital, the KGB pushed them away, not allowing them to take pictures.

As my last act of defiance, I would not let them carry me in on a stretcher. "I am going to walk in," I declared. I did, too, although vice-consul Kurt Strubel and Dr. Schadler carried my bags and walked on either side of me.

Once we reached the hospital entrance, white-coated men met us, hurried me down the hall and into a room. Several men, as many as fifteen and all wearing white coats, were waiting for me. I suspected that most of them were KGB people, but none of them said who they were. Their white coats gave the impression that they were all doctors. In fact, in these hospitals, the doctors can offer no treatment unless the KGB allows them. I noticed that the Americans had stayed—four of them—because they provided my first hope of survival.

Once inside the room, the men who looked like doctors took all my clothes off me. They treated me roughly and I felt as if, in their eyes, I was an animal, not a person. They stripped me in front of all the people there. I am sure they wanted to humiliate me. In my exhaustion, it did not bother me as much as it might have. I knew only that they didn't care and perhaps even enjoyed my humiliation.

They examined me slowly and thoroughly. "This puncture," one white-coated man touched my arm. "What is it?"

"Blood test," I managed to say through thickened lips.

"Who did it?"

"Excuse me," one of the Americans said. "Before we released her, two doctors took blood samples. First, our own doctor and then another one who flew in this morning from England. As a matter of fact, we gave her a complete physical examination before she left." He handed the man a thin file. "Here is a copy of both medical examinations, made less than an hour ago."

Even in my exhausted condition, I understood the effect of the American's words. I hoped that they did, too.

"Why did you come here?" A white-coated man's face appeared only inches from mine.

I did not answer.

"Why did you go on this hunger strike?"

"What are you trying to do?"

"Why did you come here?"

The questions continued for what seemed a long time. Either I did not answer or gave them only monosyllabic responses. First, because I had learned to be very careful in answering questions. Also, in my weakened condition, I had only enough strength to speak two or three words at a time. Despite my lack of response, they kept firing questions at me for a long time.

A psychiatrist came in, introduced himself, and said, "I want to ask you some questions. I expect to hear your answers." He quoted the saying, " 'All that glitters is not gold.' Now, do you think America is a shining country where everything is wonderful? Do you want to go there because you have heard that everything glitters? Think about those words I quoted to you. What does the saying mean?"

I hesitated in answering, knowing he would twist my words. I decided that I would give him only answers that came from the Bible. I spoke two or three words, paused, and then continued, "Some people follow the devil because he shines and makes everything seem wonderful. He is not good but he fools them."

"No, no!" he shouted. "I want you to talk about America and the Soviet Union."

"I don't want to talk about that. I want to talk about God."

"Let's try another saying." Altogether he asked me four different questions, all of them familiar sayings, and each time I gave a similar answer. When I answered, he became more angry. He also grew impatient at the slowness of my words, but I could not speak any faster. He constantly glanced back at the KGB agents who were present there. Possibly he was afraid that they did not like the way he conducted the examination.

For his last question, he mentioned another common Russian saying, " 'If you spit in the well, one day you will have to drink it.' What does that mean?"

"I don't spit in the well," I said. "But there are many people who spit on Jesus. They are wrong because he is the water of life. One day they will have to drink of that water when they stand before God because of their sins."

"Don't give me that kind of answer. You know perfectly well how to answer properly. You wish to spit at the Soviet Union. Is that it?"

Then I said, "I don't think I will ever drink of this well because I do not wish to live in the Soviet Union. I want to emigrate."

"Why do you want to leave our country?"

This time I did not answer because I had gotten away from giving him biblical answers. No matter what I said, he would attempt to twist my words and to confuse me.

I don't know if he merely grew tired of asking questions or if they felt it would do no good. He stopped pounding me with questions and abruptly left the room. A few minutes later, they put me on a special bed in an isolation ward. I heard them tell the Americans that, for now, they would not be able to see me. In truth, no one from the outside could come and talk to me.

I lay on the bed and stared at my surroundings. The other patients were elderly and most of them were dying. None of them wore clothes; they lay covered only with blankets.

They refused to let me wear any clothes, but they did give me a heavy blanket. They seemed to think that if I wore clothes I would climb out of bed, jump out of the window, and run away. I wanted to laugh at that thought because by then I didn't have enough strength left in my body to stand up. How could I think of climbing out a window?

Every hour or so someone came in, stared down at me, and asked,

"When are you going to stop this hunger strike?" It was not the same person each time but the routine seldom varied.

Because I expected them to kill me in the hospital, I wondered what difference my answers made. Why should I make it easier for them to trap me? I chose to answer no more questions.

"Will you stop now? Today?"

I closed my eyes.

"When will you stop this hunger strike?" The anger came through his voice. "When? When will you stop?"

I made no effort to let him know I understood him.

A few seconds later, I heard footsteps retreating and the closing of the door.

Not only did their persistent questions make me angry, but their refusing to allow me to wear clothes made me determined not to give in to them. I wanted to do yet more to defy them. Then I remembered something and I took my next step of defiance.

Someone at the American Embassy had packed a bag of food and sent it along with me to the hospital. To my surprise, it lay on the floor next to my bed. It took a great deal of effort to move, but I wanted to show them that I was still not going to give in, even at the point of death. I started to pull the bag up to the bed and one of the white-coated KGB men reached down and lifted it up for me. I pulled out a bag of chocolate candies. His eyes brightened, thinking I wanted to eat.

Instead, I held it out to him. "Here, take this," I said. "Good food. Good American food."

Taken by surprise, he accepted the candy. He also looked slightly embarrassed.

"More," I said. I handed him things such as candy bars, small sausages, and packages of soup.

A few minutes later, others came into the room and I continued to hand out the items, one at a time. When they saw that I actually offered American food items, not one person refused.

The real doctors (I quickly learned to distinguish them) wanted to show kindness to me, yet they did not want to displease the KGB people who watched everything they did.

One doctor said to me, "Did you see those *becov* (oxen) in the room who were wearing the white coats?"

"Yes, and I feel that all of them are not doctors."

"That is right. They are checking everything all the time. They are even checking on what we doctors are doing." He sighed. "We can do nothing without their watching us."

Because I refused to tell them that I would end the hunger strike, the second day they started to feed me intravenously. I wanted to ask, "Since you plan to kill me anyway, why does it matter?" Instead I said nothing.

"Lida Vashchenko," a white-robed KGB man said, "If you will not stop your hunger strike, we will keep this IV needle going through the night and through tomorrow. This treatment lasts only a few hours. If you stop voluntarily, we will not force-feed you any more.

For two days I held out. From time to time they would put an IV in me and when it finished, the doctor always asked, "When will you stop the hunger strike?"

On the second day I developed a high fever and chills. When an orderly reported it, the doctor rushed into the room and examined me. He was so nervous trying to get the fever down that this time he forgot to ask if I would stop the hunger strike.

I lay in the bed, praying for guidance. I did not know what to do. I was very sick and I suddenly knew that I would surely die if I continued the fast. We had come so far; could I allow it to end in death?

He left and minutes later another doctor entered the room. By this time, however, God had answered my prayer for guidance, so before he asked the usual question, I said, "Bring me soup."

A startled look appeared on his face. "You want soup?" He stared at me. "You do want soup?"

"Yes."

He turned and dashed out of the room. I could hear him as he ran down the hallway shouting, "She wants soup! She wants soup!"

A short time later somebody brought me broth and I ate every spoonful. I don't know if it was delicious or only if it had been so long since I had tasted food, I only thought it was good.

After three or four more days, they moved me to another room. With the move, they allowed me to have my clothes. To my surprise, the American officials came to see me. To my greater surprise, reporters and photographers also came in.

"Is it true?" the reporters asked. "You stopped the hunger strike?"

"Yes, it is true."

"Did they force you to stop?"

"No, I stopped by my own choice."

"Why now?"

"Because I thought it was time to stop."

Every outsider must have asked whether I voluntarily stopped the hunger strike. A few remained skeptical as though they thought the Russian government was forcing me to say "yes."

Within a week, I received a letter from Senator Carl Levin asking if I had stopped voluntarily. He had long been concerned about our family and had been supportive since our early days in the American Embassy. I told him the truth.

A few days later, I had a quiet morning with no one coming to see me. I had started to gain strength and had started back on solid food. If I ate everything the hospital people brought me, I would have put on thirty pounds. I could hardly believe the amount they brought me.

That morning a KGB man walked into the room and asked, "When we release you, what are you going to do? Go back to the Embassy?"

His question surprised me but I did not let him see that. I had expected that as soon as I was well enough to leave the hospital, they would at least take me to prison. Knowing how the system worked, I assumed they had already set up my trial. For the first time I thought that maybe they would let me go. Maybe they are afraid to harm me because of all the adverse publicity they would receive. I didn't want to presume on that, but I decided to answer as if I could do anything I wanted.

"When I leave here, I will go back to my brothers and sisters. They have been alone for four years. I want to talk to them and to explain to them what has happened." Mama and Father didn't need me, and I knew the Russian government would never let me return to the Embassy anyway. During those days while I was regaining strength, my mind centered more on the children than anything else. They were alone. I felt they needed me.

He nodded at my answer and left the room.

I heard nothing about what would happen to me. Someone from the government phoned my brothers and sisters to come to Moscow and get me. Later, I realized that the Soviets tried to use my going home as good propaganda for them. They told the people of my hometown as well as the rest of the world that I had changed my mind about my hunger strike and that I planned to return to my home in Siberia. They said that I had realized Americans were bad people and I did not want to live among them.

One morning after I had been in the hospital for two weeks, a KGB man, no longer wearing his white coat, came into the room. "Lida Vashchenko, you may go home to Chernogorsk today." He left the room without another word.

A few minutes later, two Americans came to the hospital with a car. As I got inside, one of them said, "We can take you by the Embassy to see your parents before you catch your plane. We have time to do that."

"Can I really do that?"

"Absolutely. We have permission for you to visit because we guaranteed you would not try to stay."

"No, this time I wish to go home," I said. Yet when I thought about going home, I wondered if that was a trick. Once I was out of Moscow and away from reporters, the KGB could kidnap me from the plane. They could fake an accident. They could arrest me when I got off the plane.

As I continued to think about it and pray for God's guidance, I remembered that before leaving the Embassy for the hospital, I had prayed for God to speak to me and had read:

The Lord will keep your going out and your coming in from this time forth, and for evermore. (Ps 121:8)

At that time, I had wondered if God was saying that we would not be allowed to emigrate. The more I had thought about it, the more confused I became, so I finally decided that if God was speaking to me, I did not understand the message. Now, as I sat in the Embassy car, that verse from Psalm 121 came back to me and I understood what God had meant by the words, "going out" and "coming in." I suddenly understood that God was saying that I would go out of the Embassy and then back in—even though the going back inside was temporary. In that moment, I felt a deep sense of peace inside. I had no idea what would happen, but I no longer worried. I knew that not only could I safely visit my parents at the Embassy, I also could go home to care for the rest of the family without fear.

We stopped at the Embassy. I saw my parents and then flew home. When the children saw me, the youngest hardly recognized me. I was thin, weak, and tired most of the time. For the first few days, whenever I walked to another room, Abraham (now eight) and Sarra (eleven) followed me everywhere. When I slept at night, they lay down beside me. After they fell asleep, the older ones picked them up and put them in their own beds.

After getting home, I thought and prayed about what to do next. I had fasted and that had helped, but it was not enough. We had to do something to force the Soviet government to listen more carefully and to take action on our behalf.

We talked about it a long time. We were twelve people (including Ludmilla, now part of the family) and we all had our opinions. Some wanted to do one thing, others hesitated. The younger ones didn't seem to know what to do. We finally agreed to demonstrate in front of the town officials.

I sewed together stripes of red and white to look like an American flag. Even though I had seen the American flag often during my stay at the Embassy, I could not remember the number of stars in the blue background. I made thirteen, not knowing that the first American flag looked like that. I used thirteen because of the thirteen Vashchenko children.

We made large banners with Bible verses. We also printed a sign that said we had been trying to emigrate for twenty years. Brezhnev was in power. One of the signs we made read:

Leonid I. Brezhnev,
When are you going to allow us to emigrate?

We walked right to the center of the town where the government offices are located and where people could see everything we did. Abraham and Sarra stood on either side; each carried an American flag. We marched up and down in front of the local political offices. With our tape recorder we played religious music to draw the attention of pedestrians. Many people came to watch. Some agreed with us; others yelled obscenities, a few threw stones at us. People drove up and got out of their cars. Soon even busses stopped. Everyone wanted to read our signs because people do not demonstrate in the Soviet Union, and especially not in Chernogorsk, Siberia.

Policemen tried to regulate the traffic. The obvious leader yelled, "Take your banners down and get into the bus."

We acted as if we had not heard him.

The people responded and argued among themselves. Some said, "The government should answer these people and settle their case!"

Others said, "People like that need to go to prison for causing problems."

"That one led those innocent children into doing this!" A man pointed at me. "She learned terrible things at the American Embassy and she has come back here to teach these children!"

"They only want an answer! They deserve to be heard!" A voice called out.

A fight broke out and the police rushed among the crowd to stop it. One of the policemen came over to me. "Get into the bus!"

I refused.

"Into the bus!" This time he grabbed me and pushed me toward the curb. The bus had three steps. His push made me stagger and I fell against the bottom one and badly bruised my leg.

They treated the others just as roughly. They bruised Dina's lips and Jacob's legs. The others were mostly shaken up and pushed roughly inside.

They drove us to the police station. For two or three hours they asked us question after question. Our answers remained the same. We wanted to emigrate and we were willing to do whatever was necessary to make it happen. They tried to reason with us. They argued and they scolded. They particularly ridiculed me as the leader of the demonstration. They warned me that they would not tolerate such behavior.

At times I felt afraid, but I was determined. I had watched my parents fight for their right to worship freely, and it had been denied again and again. For more than twenty years, we had begged the government to allow us to leave peacefully. Never had they listened to us. This time they would listen!

People in the Western world already knew about our plight. Organizations in England and in the United States were created on our behalf. Jane Drake, a housewife in Selma, Alabama, formed SAVE (Society of Americans for Vashchenkos' Emigration). She worked closely with Bobbette Wrample who was affiliated with a Jewish organization. The British magazine, *Buzz,* under the editor, Peter Meadows, along with Danny Smith, provided invaluable help. Michael Bourdeau and Mike Rowe of Keston College had compiled a lot of information about us and distributed it widely. The Door of Hope Ministry let people know of the desperate situation we were in. Olga and Bahoshav Hruby from New York published a journal, *Religion in Communist Dominated Lands.* Dr. Kent Hill from Seattle Pacific University, kept in personal contact with us. "Keep fighting," they all said.

In the police station I thought of all that we had gone through already. For a few seconds I wondered if it had been worth it. *Is this the way it will always be?* I asked. We try. We fight. We are so few against so many—against this powerful nation.

Then I remembered the words of my father: "One man with God is more powerful than all the evil forces in the world. One man with God can do anything."

Just hearing his words in my mind gave me new courage.

"Lida Vashchenko," the officer said. "You leave now. You take your family and go home."

Go home? Were they frightened to do anything to us? If so, it was because the people of the world were watching. With that new spark of courage, I kept my face emotionless and stared into his eyes to let him know I was not afraid. "No! You brought us here in a bus. You take us back in a bus!"

Under ordinary circumstances I would never have dared to do such a thing. But with boldness and anger mixed together, I knew I could stand up to Mr. Brezhnev himself.

He turned to another police officer and they whispered together. The other man left the room and returned shortly. "Back into the bus," he commanded.

I wanted to smile at him because I had won. But I could not do that because I might undo the victory. I had learned well to show no emotion. I only nodded and led the way. My brothers and sisters followed.

They took us home, let us out, and drove away. Of course, we did not have our banners or our tapes of Christian music. We were all exhausted from the demonstration and lay down to sleep. When we awakened, we saw that two cars had pulled up at the curb and heavily armed KGB men, dressed in uniforms, got out. They had radios and loudspeakers. They stood guard in front and back of our house. From that moment on, we were under house arrest. When any of us left home—and it had to be for a good reason—he or she went with a policeman following.

We put my homemade American flag up on the top of our roof to show that they were guarding not only us but the flag as well.

Nothing, we decided, had come out of that protest. We had to do something more drastic to call attention to our situation.

I knew exactly what to do next.

THIRTEEN

Defiant Symbol

ON APRIL 28, 1982, less than a week after our demonstration in Chernogorsk, we planned the next step. Another demonstration, but one that would have greater impact. Although under house arrest, Vera, John, Jacob, and Ludmilla escaped and traveled to the provincial capital, Krasnoyarsk. They had banners and American flags just as before. As they had expected, the police arrested them, kept them overnight, and brought them back home the following day. They threatened all of us, but we were not afraid.

They also told us that we would not be allowed to go anywhere except to stores or necessary places. However, our places of work were not considered "necessary," so that left us with no income. Fortunately, we had a good storage of staple items such as potatoes, flour, and sugar. We sold milk from our cow to get money for the day-to-day food items we needed.

In Russia, the cows all graze in a single field and one person takes care of them all. When we went to milk our cow, we passed the place where the people threw away their spoiled food. When we discovered items such as spoiled beets or other half-rotten vegetables, we took them home to eat. We fed some of them to our cow.

We raised two bulls along with our cow. One day we realized that our cow was dying because of something the people had done to her. She had been fine one day and the next she was suffering badly. We decided to kill her and sell the meat for money to buy another cow. When we slaughtered her, we found a long needle inside her stomach.

We bought another cow, but the people did the same thing again.

This time we had to kill one of the bulls to buy a cow so that we could have milk. The people also killed this cow, so we had to sell our last bull.

We kept praying, "How long, O Lord, how long?" At times we got discouraged. The children kept asking me, "How long will it be until we can be free? How long until we see Mama and Father again?"

The questions came again and again. "Do the Americans want to help us? Are we just wasting our time and making the government angry? Will they finally decide to do with us like they did with our cows?"

When I did not know how to reply or did not want to, they would say, "Lida, you have been there. You have talked to the Americans. Tell us."

I knew little more than they did, yet they seemed to think I knew much more. Many days I would be ready to say, "I can take no more." Then I would open my Bible and pray. While I can't explain it, I can only say that I would receive new strength and knew that I could go on a little longer. That is how I kept going from day to day.

Reminded of the Jews in the wilderness, I read to the family from Deuteronomy:

> "And you murmured in your tents, and said, 'Because the Lord hated us, he has brought us forth out of the land of Egypt, to give us into the hand of the Amorites, to destroy us. Whither are we going up? Our brethren have made our hearts melt, saying, "The people are greater and taller than we; the cities are great and fortified up to heaven; and moreover we have seen the sons of the Anakim there." ' Then I said to you, 'Do not be in dread or afraid of them. The Lord your God who goes before you, will himself fight for you, just as he did for you in Egypt before your eyes, and in the wilderness, where you have seen how the Lord your God bore you, as a man bears his son, in all the way that you went, until you came to this place.' " (Dt 1:27-31)

Everything had seemed as if it would work out during my days in the Embassy, yet now nothing was happening. Even as a family we could not seem to see things the same way. We were much like the

Israelites. The more I thought of it, the more discouraging it became.

One bright spot during these days was that we were able to go to the telephones at the post office when the American Embassy called us so we could speak to our parents. Local authorities told us we could not call them, but we did not have the money to do so anyway. Our parents, however, calling from the Embassy, could speak to us. We knew that the Soviets monitored our calls and sometimes cut us off in the middle of a conversation. I have always been so grateful, however, that the Americans allowed the family to call us; otherwise, we would have had no contact with them.

One of the things which most angered our neighbors was our displaying of our homemade American flag on our roof. When neighbors walked by and saw this, they yelled, "You need to go to the north and eat nothing but ice!" (By "the north" they meant the extreme region on the northern border where the state sent prisoners in exile.)

Others yelled at the brothers, "You think your sister will go to America, do you? What fools you are! You're even crazier than your sister!" They also called them all kinds of names. Because we were afraid that neighbors and townspeople would start fighting with us, we kept sticks and stones stored up by the fireplace in case we had to fight.

One day, an especially angry group of people came to the house and surrounded it. They yelled at us and their noise attracted others. At one point we could hardly hear anything but their yells and threats. It looked as if they would break in at any minute. Young Abraham began to cry, but none of us paid any attention to him because we were too concerned with the threat from outside.

Father had built a small doghouse in back of the house for our dog, Volcano. Abraham crept outside and, hidden by the fence, he crawled into the doghouse. Volcano stayed with us, barking at the unruly mob on the outside.

In the midst of all that, I prayed and thought of the story of Lot in the Old Testament. The local people surrounded his house and tried to break inside but they did not succeed. I felt that God would protect us as well.

Neighbors called the police and told them about the crowd. If the people broke into the house and harmed us, it would make the Soviets appear in a bad light, so the screaming and cursing let up when the police quickly came and ordered the people to go home. They even put several troublemakers into police cars and drove them away.

When all the people were gone, we suddenly realized that Abraham was not with us. We searched everywhere but could not find him. We opened the door to search outside. Volcano went into the yard to his house and stuck his head inside and barked. There sat Abraham with Volcano happily licking the boy's face.

We all had a good laugh, which brought relief to us after the tense situation. None of us blamed the boy for what he had done. In fact, a couple of the other children admitted that they would have done the same thing if they had thought about it.

So, the flag stayed up. But we never knew how long before the police would follow their orders to pull it down. One day a policeman finally came to the door and asked me, "Why would you put such a thing on your roof?"

"We leave it up there," I said, "because we want everyone to know that we no longer claim Russian citizenship. We have decided that this is an American home and so we put up our flag!"

The policeman's face snarled in anger. "Take it down!"

"No."

"Then we shall take it down for you."

"You are so many and very strong. How could a few children like us stop you from doing such a thing?"

That made him even more angry. He yelled commands to four policemen to climb up on the roof and remove the flag. They removed it.

After they left, local drunks yelled and challenged each other to climb up to our roof. They had seen the police do it. "We only want to follow the example the authorities set for us." One man eventually decided to climb up on the roof and another tried to stop him.

"Why do you try to stop me? Are you a Baptist, too?"

"No. Just get down."

"Get down? You are one of them! I know it! I should beat you and throw you to the Americans!"

"Good!" he yelled back in disgust. "I would love to go and live in a capitalist country!"

The man trying to climb up continued to yell angry words and the one on the ground screamed back at him. Finally, the climber jumped down and attacked him. The two of them struck blows at each other, missing as often as they hit.

Voices from the crowd yelled out, "It is a shame to have people like Vashchenkos in our Soviet country! We should take away their citizenship and throw them into the West!"

Another voice answered, "No! That's what they want. We should judge them inside this country and punish them here!"

"We plan to kill all of you Vashchenkos!" Another man who had climbed on to the roof boomed down at us. "You do nothing but bring trouble to our community!"

"We kill the big sister first! Then one by one, we take the rest of you and torture you until none are left!"

"We'll hang your bodies from the roof as a special flag to show how we deal with traitors!"

We had no idea how long that would go on or what they would do. Because of their drunken state, part of the time their threats did not make sense, but that did not make our fear of them any less real. Finally, we heard the police yelling at the five or six who by now had climbed up on the roof. "Get down! All of you and go home!"

"Go home? We have come to help. We are good citizens of the state!"

"We do not need your help! Come down!"

"Not need our help? Now you turn against us, is that it? We keep the law and now you want to protect those traitors?"

When the police threatened them with jail, the drunks turned on the police. "We wanted to help but now we see that you are working with those Baptists. We ought to kill you all."

The authorities finally made them come down from the roof and took them all away from our house. We sighed with relief that they were gone.

"But," I told the others, "this cannot be the end. If we stop now, we have accomplished nothing. Tomorrow we put up a new flag. If they take it down, we'll make another one and put it up."

The next day, police returned because neighbors had reported the presence of a new flag. "Take it down!"

"We refuse! This is the flag of our new country!"

"You are being foolish. The local people now hate you. Tonight or tomorrow or one day, they will attack you. What will happen then? We can't protect you if you keep on doing such foolish things."

"If the might of the Soviet nation cannot help us, God will have to protect us," I answered.

That answer so enraged him that he himself joined two others and they pulled down the flag. They stood in front of the house where we could see them and tore the flag into pieces. "Look at these pieces! This is to remind you that one day you will answer for this! And we will tear you to pieces," an angry voice screamed, "just as we have torn this cloth."

The police took the torn-up cloth back to the KGB office and held it as evidence against us. Later, when I spoke to the KGB officials, I saw all the pieces piled up in a box.

We knew the government was angry. Their anger only encouraged us because they did not have the authority to beat us. It did not matter that we had lost two flags. We kept making them. As soon as they took one away, we put up another. Had it not been so serious, we could even have seen it as a game.

One day, the KGB asked a relative to come to our house and to persuade us to take down the flag and to keep it down. Some of the children wanted to take it down because they did not see that it had accomplished anything. They feared the increased anger from city drunks.

The young man came to the house, but he stood outside and talked to my brothers. I heard him say that he didn't want me involved in the conversation. I peeked outside to see what was going on. I knew he could persuade them to take down the flag. I started praying, "God, please don't let us give up now. Please help us so that the flag stays up."

He explained how much better life would be for us in the community if they would only cooperate. They could return to school or go to work. They wouldn't have to stay under house arrest. He even hinted that he could help the boys find better jobs than they had had before.

They listened until our relative made one mistake. He began to use abusive language toward my brothers and said terrible things about God and the American flag. "Get out of here!" my brothers told him.

"Ha! I just spit on your God, then!" He spit at them, inflicting a great insult. It was his words and that gesture which enraged them.

I'm sure that the policemen did not understand what happened. Three policemen had been standing there, expecting that the young man and my brothers would climb up and take down the flag. So far as I know, they did not realize it was only the mistake of his insult that stopped my brothers from taking down the flag.

As he walked away, I thanked God for answering my prayer. I knew then that they could not harm us.

After that, the neighbors began to refer to our house as Little America.

As much as the flag attracted local attention, we needed to bring more widespread attention to our situation. We decided on the next step. We owned a camera and one roll of film. I wanted to take a photograph of the KGB people tearing the flag down. However, if they saw us taking a picture, they would confiscate the camera.

We had to fool them. We worked very hard and, with wood and black paint, we constructed several look-alike cameras. As soon as they came to rip down another flag, one of us ran outside and snapped a picture with the look-alike camera.

Naturally, the closest policeman grabbed the camera and threw it to the ground. The first time, the man stomped on it and stared in amazement when it fell apart. "Stupid children! It is only a toy!"

In a few minutes, another one rushed out and snapped a picture. Again, a policeman grabbed the wooden box and broke it. "A toy again!"

We kept doing it until they were convinced that we were crazy and they stopped trying to take away our toys. Then Alexander rushed out, snapped pictures with a real camera and ran back inside. Through the help of Christian friends, we had the roll developed and one clear picture turned out. He printed several copies for us.

I mailed out copies to the heads of Western nations, including America. Once I was sure they were on the way, I mailed a copy to the KGB in Chernogorsk and in Moscow. The local KGB men recognized themselves and they were so afraid that for the next eight months, they never made any further attempts to take down the flag.

Again, it seemed as if nothing was happening and I did not know what to do. I needed the wisdom of my parents, but they were still at the American Embassy. Even though I was the eldest child, at times I felt so unsure of what to do next. I had not fully recovered my strength from my hunger strike at the Embassy. Some days I was so weak I could hardly find strength to do my share of our work. When I was physically weak, I was also spiritually weak.

Then I would feel guilty for being weak. Many times, I asked God to help me because I felt stupid and ignorant. Even with the house filled with family members, many times I felt alone and in need of wisdom. "God, what shall I do next?"

One day we got a telephone call from Mama, and by then we had started using a secret code so that we could pass certain information back and forth without the KGB understanding.

Mama told me that she and Lila were going on a second fast. She asked me to join them at our home. I wanted to do anything for the family and I wanted to support what Mama was doing. Yet, this time, I did not feel right about fasting even though I agreed to join them.

The last week of June, 1982, I tried to fast. In the Embassy, we had fruit juices to take the first week while we fasted. After that I had taken only water. Here in far-off Siberia, juices were expensive and hard to find. I had so little teaching on these things and I didn't know any other way to fast. I bought juice.

I tried to explain to the others what I was going to do. They did not seem to understand—especially the younger ones. When they saw me drinking the juice, they looked upon it as special food and wanted some of it too. Naturally I shared with them. That used up the juice quickly.

The other problem involved doing my duties. When fasting I became very weak, so the children complained that I didn't do my fair amount of work. I tried to do both and I couldn't. On the other hand, I couldn't explain all of this to Mama on the phone.

I tried the fast a couple of days, quit, and then tried again. It just did not work with my trying to take care of the children. This on-off-again fast went on for nearly two months. It was a low point for me.

Another fact that hindered me was remembering what happened to me the first time. When I got to that weakest point, they took me to the hospital. In Botkin Hospital in Moscow, the Americans had stayed there as protectors. Reporters kept coming around. I was no longer in Moscow. We lived nearly four thousand miles away and who would know what was going on? The KGB could do almost anything they wanted with me and who could prove differently?

Then we heard terrible news. Mama's colitis and high blood pressure had flared up. She was very ill. I don't remember all the words they used on the phone but we knew that Mama was dying.

I do not cry easily and I didn't cry then. But inside, my heart was breaking. Mama had worked so long and so hard for freedom. Now she would not live to see it.

"Oh, God," I prayed, "don't let this happen to her. Please don't let her die yet. Not in the Soviet Union. Please."

FOURTEEN

Concern for Mama

"I WANT TO SEE MAMA AGAIN."

I don't remember which of us said that first, but it was the thought in all our hearts. Mama was dying, but she would not come home. If we wanted to see her again, we had to go to Moscow. As long as she was alive, she would not leave the Embassy unless she left it as a free woman.

We sold our fourth cow so that all of us could purchase tickets to Moscow. After buying the tickets, we went to the police headquarters.

"Our mother is dying in Moscow. We wish to visit her before she dies."

The man listened to our story, talked to someone else, and then said, "You may go but you will have to wait a few days." (Leonid Brezhnev had died two days before and Moscow was preparing for a massive funeral.) He explained that the city would be filled with people and that we would never get on a train. "Wait a few days and perhaps we can help you."

"We already have our tickets," I told him. "We are going." I had no fear of the man. The most he could do would be to refuse us the right to travel. All of us wanted to see Mama and nothing would stop us.

"Then go!" he said.

The next day we boarded the train as we had planned and arrived in Moscow three and a half days later. We notified Mama that we were coming, so we hoped someone from the American Embassy would be at the station to meet us.

A man came to us, introduced himself by name, and said, "I would like you to follow me. We will take care of you."

"Are you from the KGB?"

He did not deny it but said, "Come. Let us help you."

"If you are only going to help us get to the Embassy, then we don't need your help. We have all come here to see our mother and we do not need anything from you."

"Have it your way, then," he said, "but don't do here what you did in Chernogorsk." I knew he meant that he did not want us to demonstrate in Moscow.

I walked on past him. I did not know what would have happened if we had let him "help" us. We had one goal in mind—to see Mama—and nothing would stop us.

I went to the public telephone and called the American Embassy. I had hoped they would agree that all of us could come inside and speak with Mama. "Two at a time may come in and see her," the vice-consul said. "As soon as they come back outside, two more may go in."

"No, that isn't the way it should be," I answered. "She is very ill, is she not? You would stop all of us from being with her in her final hours?"

He tried to speak kindly to me but I would not give in on this. "No! If all of us cannot come inside and be with her, then none of us will come in and all the world will know that we could not see our parents because the American government was afraid that we would not leave the Embassy if we got inside."

Actually, both governments were afraid that, once inside, we would stay. The Americans saw no way to solve the problem. The Soviets hoped that the publicity would die down, the world would lose interest, and eventually everyone would leave. If we went inside, it would create more adverse publicity.

My words seemed to make him uncomfortable and I didn't want him to become angry. Yet we had come so far and had sold everything we had to make this trip. Because I am the daughter of both my father and my mother, I had learned to speak with a will of iron. But he pointed out that the Soviets would never allow us all to go inside.

Reluctantly, we had to agree to their terms. However, since we could not all go inside together, none of us would go inside at all. I took Sarra and Abraham with me and left the others at the train station. The three of us gathered around the basement window where Mama could see us.

It had now been nearly five years since Sarra and Abraham had seen Mama. They peered through the barred window at her. I stood next to them on the sidewalk.

Who can remember the words at that moment? It was a deeply emotional time, especially for Mama. She started to cry and I kept saying, "Don't cry, Mama. We'll all be together soon. We will, Mama! Don't cry!" She looked so sick and it must have been a terrible effort for her to stand at the window, but she didn't complain. She only talked about her illness when we asked her directly.

More than anything else I remember Mama's arm reaching out through the ornamental ironwork to touch Abraham. "You are so big now. You are no longer my little boy. You've grown up."

I could tell from his expression that he was trying hard not to cry, too.

Mama stopped crying and looked from face to face. "It will not always be this way for us," she said.

I wanted to scream from all the inner pain that had built up through the years, but I did not allow myself to do it. With the other two children around, I felt I needed to be able to comfort them. Also, with the KGB people listening behind us, I did not want to show tears which they view only as a sign of weakness.

For perhaps an hour, one by one, we each talked with Mama and Papa and our two sisters. Before we left to return to the station to pick up the others, I think I was the only one who wasn't crying.

We knew the locations of several of the registered churches in Moscow and we tried to stay at one of them. I tried the Roman Catholic, the Orthodox, and the Registered Baptist church as well as the Jewish synagogue. All of them had facilities for people to stay overnight.

Each one refused to help. "If the government will allow us to do this, we will let you stay. Otherwise we cannot help you." I suspected that the KGB had warned them that we might ask for accommodations, and they were afraid they would have trouble with the authorities if they let us stay.

Because we wanted to be near Mama and to visit her each day, it was important for us to stay in Moscow. Mama was so sick and we were convinced that unless God intervened, she would not live much longer. We had to find a place.

In desperation, we went to the apartment of one dear and brave Christian woman, Lida Staskevich, and asked her to take us in. She opened her home to us at considerable danger to herself. In Moscow, a family cannot allow you to stay unless they get permission. She broke the law by taking us in and we knew she could be heavily fined for her kindness. In some cases, they confiscate the apartment and make the family leave Moscow.

That night a plan had begun to form in my head but I knew I would have to convince the others. "We can't get inside to see Mama," I said, "and I'm not going to just sit here and then just go back home. We must do something else. Something to call the world's attention to our situation."

I argued and discussed the matter with them for a long time. The younger children had not gone through the years of suffering that Luba, Nadia, and I had. They had never done much in the way of active resistance to the authorities.

I remembered the words of the KGB man at the train station. He warned us because he didn't want us to demonstrate. If the possibility of our demonstrating would bother him or even make him afraid, it indicated that those higher up were afraid. Finally, I said, "To challenge them with banners, as we had done before, could be the most powerful thing that we, a small group of people, can do." I finally persuaded the others to agree.

We made banners with messages asking for our freedom to emigrate. We carried the banners rolled up until we came to the busy intersection near the KGB headquarters. The boys did not like this idea and kept saying that the KGB would never allow a handful of people to march around with anti-Soviet slogans. Although they thought we were wrong and they would not carry any signs, they agreed to walk behind us and carry our suitcases.

At the intersection, we stopped long enough to unfold our banners. We knew that if we waited until we got right in front of the KGB building, they would run outside and snatch the banners out of our hands. We lined up like a small army, began to sing, and marched across the street.

By the time we crossed the street, crowds had started to gather and cars were stopping so people could see what was going on. Officials from the KGB building rushed outside.

"Take down those banners!"

"We can't!" I yelled back. "We are waiting for reporters who will be coming in a few minutes to take our pictures!"

The expression on his face changed from a scowl to a question, as if he did not know whether to believe me. He seemed unsure of what to do next, so we kept parading back and forth. He watched a few more seconds before he called others outside. They discussed the situation heatedly before they took action. Within minutes they confiscated the banners and arrested all of us.

Our brothers, who stood along the curb with the luggage, had not marched in front of the KGB and they assumed they would not be involved. However, that didn't save them because the KGB arrested them as well.

They brought us into an office and asked us questions. We tried to be frank, saying as we always did, that we wanted to emigrate. After a long time, they put us all into one room. "You will be staying here a long time," a uniformed man said. "If you have any money, I will send someone to buy food. If not, you will have nothing to eat here."

Even though they talked roughly, they did nothing to harm us physically. As soon as I realized this, I knew we had an advantage. They were more afraid of us now than we were of them. Even though we were prisoners, I felt a flush of victory. They would not harm us—they did not dare. Because I did not know if the room was bugged (although I assumed it was), I whispered to the children and we decided to make the most of our time there.

Since they were uncomfortable with us and maybe even afraid, we would keep them aware of our lack of fear. We started to sing hymns—loudly.

Two or three times, someone came into the room and shouted, "Too much noise. Stop that singing!"

We obediently stopped and even smiled innocently. As soon as the door closed, we began again. After awhile they stopped coming in.

Later that afternoon, just before dark, a uniformed man came inside. "We have no food here. If you have money, we can send someone to buy it for you. Otherwise—"

"We would not want to make the government pay for our food," I said. We still had a little money left and we gave it to him. True to their word, they brought us food to eat. When we were not eating, we sang Christian songs. Other prisoners heard us and came as close to the room as they could. So did people who worked in the building. Sometimes we could hear voices. Some encouraged us and others mocked us. We kept on singing.

One of the KGB people said, "We need to keep you Vashchenkos eating all the time. That is the only time we can have any quiet."

We laughed but that also made me feel good. We determined to make them know we would not give up. As long as we were awake, we sang all the songs we knew.

We were kept in that room four days. Our parents did not know what happened to us. They called the reporters and told them we were missing. The reporters started asking questions. Even the ambassador got involved and investigated our disappearance. Eventually they located us.

The KGB then released us and put us on a plane back to Chernogorsk.

When we returned home, one of the first things we did was to put up the American flag again, but for the next three months, nothing new developed. It made me wonder many times if anything would ever happen. Despite my doubts, I knew I had to keep holding on.

In March, 1983, a little more than a year after I left the American Embassy, I had the worst case of flu in my life. For days I could not get out of bed. Gradually I started to improve. On my first full day out of bed, someone came to our door. I recognized her from the Chernogorsk office where they issued visas. She was alone so I opened the door. She did not introduce herself, but stood in the doorway, and said one sentence to me. "Now you must come to the *OVIR* (immigration) office."

"For what purpose?"

She turned and walked away.

I had been tricked so many times, I did not know what this would mean. Yet I had a sense that it would be different this time.

When I appeared the next day, they told me to fill out forms and to apply for an exit visa from the Soviet Union. "You may apply for either West Germany or Israel." I chose Israel.

I could tell by the surprised look on their faces and by the way they talked that they had never expected this to happen. I did exactly as they told me, filled out the forms, and turned them in.

Less than a week later, the same woman official called me to her office where she informed me, "On April 10, you will leave for Krasnoyarsk."

She did not tell me that I would leave the country from Krasnoyarsk. I hoped that I could go but I did not know. I started asking questions.

"You may go home now," the person in charge said.

"I don't want to leave the country alone," I persisted. "We want the whole family to go."

"You have been asking to leave for a long time. We are going to allow you to leave."

I knew then that they were not tricking me this time. But for me to leave without the others was not the victory I wanted. "But I don't want to go alone."

"I can do nothing about this. These are our orders from Moscow and we follow them. The Kremlin has arranged for you to buy the tickets and we can change nothing."

I went home perplexed, wondering what all of this meant. I talked with the other children and they felt I should go. I didn't want to go. I cried and cried because I did not want to leave them.

"But if you go . . . " they kept saying.

"It may be the beginning for all of us."

We finally decided that if the government allowed me to leave, I should go. I could then help the rest of the family from the outside.

During the waiting period, I could not sleep. I cried frequently and felt as if my heart was broken. I constantly questioned God. "Why did you do this to me? I wanted to leave but not this way. Not alone without the others."

I talked with people from our church and told them I would be leaving on April 10. They were excited for me and decided to gather together on that day and see me off. Somehow the government office found out what we were planning to do.

Early on the morning of April 5, the same woman from the visa office came to the house again. "Lida Vashchenko, tomorrow you will go to Krasnoyarsk. You will take all of your clothes with you. You will also go alone."

"I will not go alone."

"The Kremlin has ordered only one ticket."

"I don't care. I will not go alone."

She walked away.

That evening we bought tickets for the train so that Vera and John could go with me to Krasnoyarsk. The three of us traveled there together on the evening train, a journey of nearly ten hours.

The next morning we went to the Krasnoyarsk government office together. They had more forms for me to fill out. They sent me from building to building for different forms and to have copies made of the forms I had already filled out. It took up most of the day.

I had no papers of my own, such as a birth certificate, so they told me that anything I needed I could get in Washington, D.C., in the Soviet Embassy.

"No," I said, "I don't want to go the Soviet Embassy or see the Soviet authorities again. You should provide me with such papers."

"Don't you want to have Soviet citizenship when you get to the West?"

"No," I said as firmly as I could, staring into his face. "I don't want Soviet citizenship."

He merely shrugged his shoulders but said nothing more. Minutes later they handed me papers to sign that said I knew they had stripped me of my citizenship. For my final instruction, they told me that I must go to the airport for a flight to Moscow.

That night the three of us flew from Krasnoyarsk to Moscow. The American vice-consul, Kurt Strubel, who had been helpful to me before, pulled up on the runway of the airport in a car. He drove me to a place in the center of Moscow where I picked up my ticket to Vienna. My ticket had already been paid for by people from the West and no one explained who gave the money.

Although I knew I was leaving sometime that day, I naturally wanted to see my parents, but the authorities would not let me. "There is no time for that." They took me to what I think was the Dutch Embassy that handled the affairs of Israel. I had to fill out more papers. I knew then that I was getting closer to leaving the Soviet Union. No matter what doubts I had before, they were gone now. I would soon leave.

I still had a sense of sadness because I knew I would be going alone. As I went through everything I had to do, I kept praying silently that my emigration would be the first one, but not the only one.

That afternoon at 2:00, I boarded the plane for Vienna. I paused and looked back at Vera and John. It was a sad moment for me as well as a moment of great joy. I could finally leave after waiting more than twenty years. But I had no assurance that I would ever see the members of my family again.

I wanted to run back and beg that at least Vera and John might be allowed to go with me. But I knew it would have done no good. It was settled and I was leaving.

Alone.

FIFTEEN

Final Victory

WHAT WOULD LIFE BE LIKE outside the Soviet Union? How many times had I wondered? How many times had I tried to imagine it? How could my freedom be good if the others could not share it? Americans had talked to me often of their life, but it still had not become clear. They told me about having the freedom to go anyplace, anytime and about never being spied upon or questioned by authorities. I still could not comprehend it because I had no experience to compare it with.

Yet as the plane took off from Moscow's Domodidovo Airport, I could not think of anything except my family remaining in Russia.

I was thankful for Ray Barnett, Mike Rowe, and Danny Smith who traveled with me from Moscow. Their presence brought me peace and they sensed my sadness at leaving the others behind.

As the plane became airborne, I felt a great surge of assurance. In the company of three foreigners, I knew I would not be turned back.

When our plane landed at Vienna, the pilot called out my name on the intercom and said, "A car from the American Embassy is waiting for you."

I saw a large black car flying the American flag on the hood parked a short distance from the plane. The door opened and a man stepped out. He came toward me, his hand outstretched. "I'm Jim Hughes." He was big, dark, tall, and sounded American. I knew from his first words that he was a kind man. He escorted us through customs and helped us move quickly through all the paperwork.

I phoned my parents from Vienna and they were overjoyed that I had reached Austria safely. Father said, "Lida, you are now on the top of a hill. You can see things much better from there than we can from the basement window. You are free and you will know what to do. We are still here and do not know what to do next."

I wanted to burst into tears but held myself back. They had stayed in the Embassy such a long time and now I was free. They did not know what to do next. I tried to encourage them, reminding them that I would work hard until their turn came to emigrate.

"Even now we are hearing rumors that the Americans want us to leave here," he said, "and that they will stop working to help solve our problem. What do you think we should do, Lida?"

"I don't know," I said. "I am out of Russia but I don't know anything new." I had only been out of the country a few hours and I didn't want to give them any wrong advice.

"But you can talk to people, many people. You can ask their advice and then tell us if we should go back to Siberia."

"But I still do not know what to tell you," I said.

We talked about other things then and before we hung up, Father said, "Someone has just come here to the Embassy from America. I think he has a message about us from President Reagan. We can see him tomorrow—Dr. Robertson from Vermont."

It was about nine o'clock that night when I finished speaking with them. I promised that I would give them some kind of answer the next morning.

A little later I tried to go to bed but I could not. I felt so heavy in my heart for the rest of my family. I was free but if they were not also out of Russia, what good was it for me?

What should I tell them? I prayed and received no answer. I did not want to give them wrong advice and take the responsibility for their decision. I prayed and my prayers met with silence. I did not know what to do.

I finally lay on the bed but I could not sleep, even though I was tired. When my eyes closed, all I could see was Father and Mama in the basement room. Finally, I must have fallen asleep because it was early in the morning when I opened my eyes again.

"God," I pleaded, "you are asking of me more than you asked of Abraham. You told him to take his one son and offer him as a sacrifice. You ask me to sacrifice fifteen people. How can I do this? I do not know what to say to them."

Wearily I grabbed my Bible. In the past when I have been confused and God has not given me an answer, I have opened my Bible at random and read the first verse my eyes fell upon. In desperation, I decided to try it again.

I read these words:

> Yet now take courage, O Zerubbabel, says the Lord; take courage . . . take courage all you people of the land, says the Lord; work, for I am with you, says the Lord of hosts, according to the promise that I made you when you came out of Egypt. My Spirit abides among you; fear not. (Hg 2:4–5)

After I read the verse several times, I understood what God wanted to say to me. We should all continue to work for their emigration. I also had the strong impression to tell my parents that they should leave the Embassy, return home, and continue to work to leave the country.

The next morning that is the message I gave them. That same day Dr. Robertson flew from Moscow to Vienna to see me. "I spoke with your parents," he said, "and I want you to know that President Reagan wants to help. We do not know what the Soviet government will do, but we still want to help any way we can."

As I listened to him, I realized that even a man as powerful as the American president could not assure us that the Soviet government would release the whole family. I knew once again that we had only one unfailing source.

After Dr. Robertson left, I prayed.

A few days later, I flew on to Tel Aviv with Ray Barnett, Danny Smith, and Mike Rowe. We arrived in Israel at the time of the Jewish Passover, April 12, 1983. The government, strict about observing their holy day, do not open their offices. I do not know any details except that through the intervention of the Americans, the immigration people met me at the airport and opened their office there long enough to issue me a three-month visitor's visa.

Once finished, we walked into the terminal. Christians who live in Israel had been waiting to meet me. I met an American representative from the United Pentecostal Church, Rev. N.A. Urshan. Keston College sent Mike Bordeaux. Maria Keller of the Door of Hope personally handed me tickets for the rest of my trip. Dozens of reporters showed up and kept me so busy asking questions and talking to me, that I had little time to get lonely. It made the parting from my family easier. I was nervous, happy, excited, and confused. My English failed me and so did words from my own tongue. I felt foolish and wanted to say so much but I did not know how. Finally, I made a brief statement. "I am thankful that Israel has allowed me to enter and I hope they will give the same permission to my family."

A full month passed before I received the exciting news that I had been waiting for: my entire family had permission to leave the Soviet Union. They would also go to Vienna as I had done. Kind people from the West again came to my financial support and paid for my ticket to meet them in Vienna.

My family came out of Russia with only their few personal possessions. They left behind their Bibles and other religious materials. The Christians still in the Soviet Union needed them more.

When they deplaned, I could hardly believe my eyes. How can words ever describe that moment of joy for us? When I saw Mama and Father walking toward me, followed by my brothers and sisters and Ludmila, it was the single, most happy moment in my entire life. We had prayed and dreamed for it so long. Now it was reality. We embraced; we laughed; we shed tears; we didn't ever want that moment to end.

We talked and talked, going over the preparations for the trip from Vienna to Israel. I didn't want to part from them for even a few minutes. The moment was too wonderful to let go. After a few days together in Vienna, we all boarded a plane together. On Tuesday, June 29, the family arrived in Israel.

The Washington Post featured an article about the family when they left Russia. They referred to it as "the end of an extraordinary diplomatic episode that was an embarrassment for the Soviet Union and an awkward problem for the United States."

One day an official asked me to come to his office in the American Embassy in Tel Aviv. Not knowing why they called me, I felt quite nervous. The man who asked me to come introduced himself as Shuly Wise. He spoke Russian, Hebrew and English. He made me feel comfortable by telling me his own story. While still in his teens, he had tried to leave Russia after World War II. Along with seventeen other Jewish boys who feared the communist oppression if they remained, they set out for the West. Fifteen of them were killed and only Shuly Wise and one other person made it to freedom.

Because of his terrible ordeal, he easily understood what we had gone through. I relaxed and we talked freely for several minutes. After telling me how happy he was that our family had been able to leave the Soviet Union, he said, "The Chmykhalov family still wants to emigrate."

I felt a tightening in my stomach. Our two families had all belonged to the same church since the Chmykhalovs joined in 1954. We had worshiped together and prayed together many times. We had supported each other through sieges of persecution and ridicule. During our days in the American Embassy in Moscow, however, our relationship changed. First, it was merely a drifting apart. Then we began to dislike each other. It was not a matter of who was right and who was wrong. When seven people, members of two families, must live twenty-four hours a day for five years in one room, it naturally causes tensions between them.

We were all worried about what would happen to us and what would happen to our families. Maria and her son were with us now in Israel, but her husband and the other children had stayed in Chernogorsk.

Some days we argued over small things that built into big issues. At other times we remained silent in the others' presence, avoiding even looking at each other. Jealous feelings took over several times when one family received more attention than the other. At times I did not like Maria Chmykhalov and felt she did not like me. I frequently felt guilty over the way things went. In my mind, I kept thinking that we ought to be able to live in that crowded space and not fight among ourselves. But we were also very human.

"The Soviet government will not release the Chmykhalov family unless you extend an invitation to them," he said. "Will you do that? Will you sign for them?"

I knew that the Chmykhalovs who remained in the Soviet Union had received many invitations to America just as we had. Then I understood why the Soviet officials insisted on that single condition. They obviously knew of our bickering and arguing while living together in that basement room. Stalling for time so that I could think more clearly, I asked, "Why me? I am nobody to give them an invitation."

"If it does not come from you, the Soviets will not accept it from anybody."

The knot in my stomach tightened and my head began to ache. My first reaction was to refuse to help. Immediately, I thought of the unkind things Maria had said and done (and forgot what we had said and done to her, of course). I paused to pray silently to know what to do.

Then I remembered an event from years before. When I ran away with baby Aaron and no one wanted to offer us shelter, Maria Chmykhalov opened her house and endangered her family. I had asked God for an opportunity to repay her kindness. Now I had the chance to do that. God, why do you do this now? When we were friends, it would have been easy. Now that we have become enemies, I don't want to do it. I argued in my mind with God, yet all the time, I knew what I must do.

"Yes, of course, I will sign the invitation," I said calmly and looked at Mr. Wise. I don't think he knew the great turmoil I had to go through before I could speak those words.

Three weeks after my family came out, I felt a deep gratitude to God and happiness that all thirteen members of the Chmykhalov family also received their freedom. Through the help of Frieda (Mrs. Gordon) Lindsay of Christ for the Nations, they went to St. Louis and then to Dallas, Texas.

My family found the country of Israel as beautiful as I had. But we knew that we could not stay indefinitely. They were kind enough to extend our visas until we made our plans.

We faced a few days of uncertainty about our future, but we had been through so much by then that nothing seemed impossible to us. Again, Ray Barnett came to our aid. He told us that the mother of his secretary, Susan Nelson, owned a house in Seattle, Washington. He arranged for us to fly to Seattle and live in that house for two weeks while her mother was away. That gave us time to settle and make decisions about the future.

For the first time in our lives, we were free.

Epilogue

MY FAMILY SETTLED IN Washington state. The younger ones entered school. They have made many friends and love their new country. Only one sad event happened through all of this. On October 21, 1985, my father, Peter Vashchenko, died of cancer.

To remember his death still causes me pain. He was not a perfect man or father. Yet he sincerely loved God and he was a man of strong convictions. He would never compromise on anything he believed in. Like any daughter, I had moments when I felt angry or disappointed in him. Yet he was such a strong man who greatly shaped my life. Only after his treatment in the psychiatric hospital did we grow apart. They took part of the real Peter Vashchenko away.

Yet, in my heart, I can remember my father from before the hospital days. He taught me so much by his simple words and his concern for me. Because of his life and his courage, I, too, learned to stand up to the powerful state of the USSR. He gave us the vision of freedom. Our present freedom is the greatest heritage he could leave us.

Recently, my secretary, Marlene Rice, wondered why I did not fear for my life because the KGB had boasted that they could kill me at any time they chose to do so—wherever I was. She was curious as to why I was not afraid to die at their hands. I did not have to think long for an answer. It is simply better to die saying something for God, than to live saying nothing at all.

A Final Word from Lida

Today I am working on behalf of an organization I founded, Set Them Free. I am deeply concerned and want to assist other Christians in the world who are behind the iron curtain.

After twenty-three years of waiting, struggling, praying, and enduring, our family emigrated from the USSR. This came about mainly through the publicity and pressure put upon both the American and Russian governments through free-world articles and media coverage. Many signed petitions to let these governments know that we are concerned about religious persecution in communist countries.

We continue to send requests to the First Secretary of the USSR, requesting that the Soviet government comply with the charter of human rights that they signed along with thirty-five other countries.

We are doing what we can to make the rest of the world know of the religious oppression within the Soviet Union. Thousands of other Christians want to emigrate because they cannot worship freely in their own country. These are the people I am trying to help.

You can help, too!
- By writing letters
- By signing petitions (we will supply them upon request)
- By praying for Christians behind the iron curtain
- By prayer and financial support of Set Them Free.

Contact me through:
Set Them Free
P.O. Box 2520
Orange, CA 92669

Other Books of Interest
from Servant Books

Divine Appointments
Larry Tomczak

Everyday miracles can happen to every Christian willing to trust God and surrender fully to him. God has an agenda for his people if his people are willing to respond to the call in Scripture to do the works of Jesus, in the church and in the world. $5.95

Chasing the Dragon
Jackie Pullinger

God called Jackie Pullinger to Hong Kong's infamous Walled City, a haven of filth, crime, and sin. There she spoke of Jesus to brutal hoods and they were converted, to prostitutes who then retired from their trade, and to heroin junkies who miraculously found a new power that freed them from the bondage of drug addiction. Here is her amazing story—exactly as it happened. *$3.95*